ADVANCE PRAISE FOR

WILD WRITING WOMEN
Stories of World Travel

"Fascinating and scrupulously crafted tales of exploits, encounters and accidents that few men could or would undertake or experience with such grace and good humor."
—Simon Winchester, author of *The Professor and the Madman*

"The most distinctive and appealing travel anthology of the year."
—Tim Cahill, author of *Pass the Butterworms: Remote Journeys Oddly Rendered*

"These gutsy women have traveled to the far corners of the earth and their intrepid tales push the envelope in adventure, romance, and humor!"
—Marybeth Bond, author of *Gutsy Women: More Travel Tips and Wisdom for the Road*

"Their on-the-road lessons range far beyond gender and geography to touch the very heart of why we travel, and who we are."
—Don George, editor of Salon.com's *Wanderlust*

WILD WRITING WOMEN
Stories of World Travel

LISA ALPINE

JACQUELINE HARMON BUTLER

LAUREN CUTHBERT

LYNN FERRIN

CARLA KING

JENNIFER LEO

DANIELLE MACHOTKA

LINDA WATANABE MCFERRIN

PAMELA MICHAEL

CATHLEEN MILLER

CHRISTI PHILLIPS

ALISON WRIGHT

The Globe Pequot Press

GUILFORD, CONNECTICUT

To Don George,
for bringing us together

Previously published in 2001 by Wild Writing Women Press

Text design by Christi Phillips

Manufactured in the United States of America
First Globe Pequot Edition/First Printing

Contents

foreword

People tell tales about writers' groups—about competition, hostility, lack of focus. We can tell you this: Find people whose spirit you enjoy; share your work, your heart and your dreams with them, and you will have friends for life.

The members of Wild Writing Women hail from a variety of backgrounds and our ages span four decades. But the traits that bind us together are a love of travel and adventure and a compulsion to record our experiences for others. Throughout the eight years we've been meeting consistently, our paths have crisscrossed the globe—from the lonely roads of Inner Mongolia to the bat caves of Central America, from the gambling palaces of Las Vegas to the Australian outback. The one place our journeys always converge, however, is at our WWW third-Wednesday-of-the-month meetings, open to any of us who happen to be in town that week. There we've polished our skills, developed our confidence, found first homes for our stories and cheered one another's successes. Most of all, our meetings give us a chance to connect and to share our work with other women travelers and writers.

Then there's the intimacy, the camaraderie that comes only after years of fellowship and familiarity. Not only have we nurtured each other's writing, we've also nurtured each other— through an overseas bus accident, a breast cancer operation, a critically ill child, empty bank accounts, a broken wrist, broken romances, broken dreams and the rejection of editors who we all felt needed something broken.

The origin of our name, Wild Writing Women, is mired somewhere in the mists of memory, Merlot and myriad word games that swirl around a particular San Francisco bar. The London Wine Bar, located in the Financial District, has long been a hangout for the group. There we've raised a few glasses in celebration, brainstormed, argued, entertained favorite editors, hosted an annual Winter Solstice get-together and even kicked off a round of spontaneous dancing, much to the surprise of the Wine Bar's regular stock exchange patrons. One evening, somewhere in between toasting our adventures and planning a still-yet-to-be-consummated group excursion to Tibet's Mount Kailas, word games surrounding the letter "W" ended with a moniker that stuck: Wild Writing Women.

The composition of our group has fluctuated over the years, evolving and changing along with our members. Today, however, we stand at twelve, a number said to be best for mastermind groups and just one short of a traditional coven.

Wild Writing Women: Stories of World Travel is an expression of our work and of our friendship. Many of the stories included herein debuted at a WWW meeting, some to acclaim, others to hard-nosed criticism, all to appreciation and respect. Producing our anthology has been quite a journey. It was, in fact, a little like trying to navigate the Grande Corniche in a tank. But we got through it, as we get through most things, with a sense of humor, and a pen in one hand and a glass of wine in the other.

Wild Writing Women
www.wildwritingwomen.com
San Francisco, California
May 2001

Introduction

I first met Linda Watanabe McFerrin at Book Passage's Travel Writers Conference in Corte Madera, California. She was also on the faculty and she seemed rather shy, a little uncertain. Later that night, sitting outside the bar drinking martinis, I quickly revised my opinion. I recognized a sly sense of humor, a poet's soul, a deep intelligence, and the ability to match me drink for drink and stay upright. We had fun. We met annually after that, always at Book Passage and, to be honest, she was much of the reason I kept going. I enjoyed catching up with all the great people who help make the Book Passage conference one of the most fun gatherings of travel people there is, but I always hoped Linda would be there.

We got to know each other and started meeting for lunch on the occasions I was in San Francisco on business. My affection for her deepened, as did my respect for both her writing and her work ethic. Linda continually strives to build and extend her considerable skills and also to pass on what she has learnt to others; she is a wonderful teacher. However, as much as I love Linda, her greatest gift to me has been introducing me to the wonderful, fabulous women who make up the WWW writers' group. I can only say that getting to know Alison, Jacqueline, Carla, Danielle and the rest of the gals has been a delight and a privilege, and the evenings I have spent with various combinations of this group have been some of the best times I have had. Not only are they outrageous, honest, fun and, well, wild, they are also people with a real lust for life and the courage to insist that life deals with them on their terms.

All of travel's great moments are here in this book: the little moments which change your life, the small triumphs, the huge adventures that you recount years later and think, "Did I really do that?" Travel heightens all the senses. At home the days speed by, each taken up with the business of living, but the moment you leave the everyday behind, anything and everything is possible. These stories encapsulate so well the sense of freedom and potential that every trip carries within it. From Jacqueline playing the seductress in France or Lauren playing with fire at a volcano's edge to Carla confounding everyone as the tall, slim, beautiful blonde who rides "big" bikes in unbelievable places, these amazing women show us that with self-belief and good humor you can tackle anything.

Of course, travel isn't always grand adventure—and sometimes we have to travel simply to see ourselves more clearly or to discover that home is not necessarily where we happen to be living, as Jennifer and Danielle reveal so poignantly. You can see the expected sights from a completely unexpected angle, like Pamela. While Cathleen and Christi powerfully—and rather spookily—remind us that not everything we see need necessarily be confined to the known sights of this physical world.

And then there is the brave, terrible story from Alison. Ali the intrepid, who has spent her life documenting the disappearing cultures of the world on film. She isn't tall, and she is only slightly built, but by sheer force of will she summoned all her faith and belief to keep living after a horrific bus accident in Laos almost killed her. In the face of a long arduous trek back to health, Ali has amazed us all with her refusal to accept any restrictions on her travel and her life, and her indomitable spirit has awed everyone who knows her. Together we have had so much fun. We've talked for hours, soaked in hot Japanese baths, drunk far too much wine, been lost and found. Ali, the mere possibility that we almost lost you has made me realize how precious friends are and how one must never take them for granted.

Travel is an addiction, and it is very difficult to maintain and sustain relationships when you are obsessed with going away unless, of course, you are lucky enough to share your passion with a partner. Writing is also a solitary profession and it is no accident that travel writing traditionally has been seen as the preserve of men, the "rugged-individual-seeking-adventure" type, rather than a career for women. Lynn's hilarious account of what can happen when a woman finds herself in the world of the rugged-individual-seeking-adventure type still makes me laugh when I remember it. "Normal" women don't leave their families, their friends or their lovers. They don't seek a career that takes them out into the world and back to spend long hours locked up in a room with their computer unless, of course, like Lisa, they find themselves having to play mother in the depths of the Amazonian jungle. Women are supposed to be available to those they love and who love them; they are not supposed to be restless, itinerant spirits, traveling wherever the whim takes them. Of course there have been many women travel writers, but in order to pursue success in their careers they have had to sacrifice much and, with dogged determination, cling to their belief in themselves and their right to live as they choose.

While these stories don't dwell on the obstacles that the writers have had to overcome in order to write them, it is not hard to perceive the spirit, passion and determination which suffuses them. Many of these women have faced great trials in their lives, but to sit with them and listen to them tell their stories, whether of travel or just some daily, domestic trial, recounted with a wry smile or infectious laugh, is to recognize their strength and their determination to wring every drop from every day.

All these women have stories and all are inspiring. Their love of travel, their refusal to accept for themselves what so many people call "real life," meaning "everyday life," and their ability to find adventure and meaning wherever they go show us how many dimensions there are to adventure and how it is to be found in the smallest of actions—from a glance, to a motorbike ride across China. I can only say, "Well done, Wild Writing Women, long may you continue to go and come back and be available for each other—and for me!"

Maureen Wheeler
Lonely Planet Publications
Footscray, Australia
May 2001

Up Mandalay Hill

LAUREN CUTHBERT

For the wind is in the palm-trees, an'
the temple-bells they say:
'Come you back, you British soldier;
. come you back to Mandalay!'
— Rudyard Kipling

When I was a child, I was fascinated by maps,
even more by the names on the maps.

Antigua, Jakarta, Zanzibar, Shanghai.

Mellifluous, mysterious words, words full of promise, words that
beg to be read aloud. They slip off the tongue, as smooth and rich
as a fine wine, hanging lightly in the air, a liquid song, seducing
first the ear, then the mind.

Bahia, Sahara, Kashmir, Calais.

My grandmother, who lived in India in the 1930s and who
traveled by ship from San Francisco to get there, stopping at nearly
a dozen ports along the way, encouraged my verbal wanderlust.

For my eighth birthday she bought me a stand-up globe, brightly colored and bumpy with topographical markings. I spent hours spinning it round and round, my index finger lightly pressed against the plastic so that the Himalayas, the Andes, the Rocky Mountains massaged the tip as they whirled by. Once the orb slowed to a halt, I'd lift my finger and pronounce the name of whatever lay below—spinning again if I landed on water or someplace I already knew—twisting my tongue around the unfamiliar, tasting the sounds.

Madagascar, Mykonos, Sofia, Versailles.

But the name that called out to me most, soft poetry in its voice, was Mandalay. I loved the feel of the word as much as its lyrical sound, the way it rolled along my tongue, languid and delicious.

Looking at Mandalay on the globe, set smack-dab in the middle of upper Burma, I determined to visit one day. And I knew, as only an eight-year-old can know such things, that I would love it.

But when I finally got to Mandalay, some twenty years later, I did not love it at all.

The country's second largest city, Mandalay was the site of the last royal capital before the British colonized Burma—now called Myanmar by its military government—in 1885. Today it remains the nation's cultural center, the most "Burmese" of cities.

When I arrived, however, culture was the last thing on my mind. Much of my body was covered with the red, itchy rash of prickly heat (the result of four glorious but baking-hot days cycling the pagoda-speckled plain of ancient Pagan) and I cared only about finding an air-conditioned hotel. There is little treatment for prickly heat beyond transfer to a cool climate. In mid-July, Mandalay, sprawled across the dusty region of the upper Irrawaddy River, is anything but cool.

Worse, by the time I collected my bag from the airport tarmac and headed out to find a taxi, there were none left. Unlike the other tourists on the flight from Pagan to Mandalay, all of whom were met by officials of Myanmar Travels and Tours, the government tourist agency, I was traveling independently—not the easiest way to get around.

I approached one of the airport officials. Where could I find a taxi?

"No taxis," he said. "They are all taking tourists to their hotels."

Would they return to the airport when they were done? He shook his head no; they would not return again until the following day.

He suggested I hail a passing bus. "Maybe one will take you to your hotel," he offered.

I stood under the blazing noon sun along the dusty road outside the airport, my backpack slumped against the trunk of a withered palm tree. I saw nothing that looked like a bus, only modified vans, belching smoke and heavy with human cargo. People stared as they passed. A trail of sweat inched down my back. My rash burned an angrier shade of red.

Soon enough, curiosity got the better of two pedestrians. They wandered over and one of the men spoke to me in Burmese. I pulled out my map and pointed to the location of the Mandalay Hotel, my best bet, I'd been told, for air conditioning. The man motioned back toward the airport.

"Taxi," he said, smiling heartily. I shook my head no.

The two conferred a moment. Then, with another big smile, the man stepped out into the street and flagged down one of the passing vans.

It was crammed well beyond capacity, easily one of the most crowded I'd seen. People hung off the back. They spilled from the sides. Five or six men were balanced on the roof, fingers wrapped around frayed ropes tied to the side of the truck.

The man consulted with the driver. He, in turn, stuck his head out the window and called out to the back of the truck. A loud chorus ensued. Suddenly, a shaved head popped out from the rear of the vehicle.

"Where you go?" asked the monk, in broken but definite English. I told him. He yelled to the driver. The driver yelled back. More deliberation. Finally, the monk turned to me again, waving a bare, tattooed arm.

"Come," he said. "The driver will take you."

Given the discussion that had greeted my answer, I very much doubted that the hotel was on the regular route, but I wasn't about to argue. A man standing on the pavement grabbed my pack and threw it onto the top of the truck. I headed for the back of the truck but was waved away and ushered to the cab. One of the three men seated there hopped out and clambered up onto the roof. With much grinding and clanking, we set off.

Twenty minutes later, the truck pulled up outside my hotel. I paid what seemed a paltry sum for door-to-door service and checked in. After a cold shower—generally the only kind in Burma, though in my case it was welcome—I set out to see the city.

I toured the remains of the reconstructed Royal Palace, which burned to the ground in 1945 when British troops bombarded the fortress, then held by the Japanese. I admired the Shwenandaw monastery, part of the old Palace complex, and one of the few original wooden buildings still standing. I visited the Mahamuni Pagoda, Mandalay's most important religious structure, and watched the faithful paste tissue-paper-thin strips of gold leaf to the twelve-foot-high Buddha housed within, adding to the two-inch-thick layer that already coated the image.

Midway through the second day, however, I gave up. Despite the many sights left to see, my fiery skin dictated leaving for a cooler locale. The next morning, I decided, I would do as the colonial British had done and escape to the old hill station of Maymyo, set high in the foothills of the Shan Plateau.

So, as the afternoon drew to a close, I headed toward Mandalay Hill, the city's most famous attraction. It was from the top of the hill that the Buddha was said to have prophesied that a great city would be founded below. It is also the only site offering a wide-angle view over the otherwise pancake-flat terrain.

Climbing almost 775 feet above the surrounding plain, Mandalay Hill is cut by covered stairways, each with numerous small temples scattered along the path. Under the stern gaze of the carved white *chinthes*—talisman lion-griffins that guard all temples, ensuring, among other things, that visitors remove their shoes before entering sacred ground—I slipped off my sandals and headed for the stairs. Seated on a stone bench at the base of the path was a lone, saffron-robed monk. He stood as I started up the stone stairway and fell into step beside me.

After ten days in Burma, I was used to uninvited company. The country is not often included on the itinerary of travelers to Southeast Asia; those who do visit attract considerable attention. As a woman traveling alone, I attracted even more.

This time, however, I preferred to walk by myself. I increased my pace. Without seeming to hurry, my companion matched my step. I gradually fell back. So did he. I stopped, pretending to retrieve something from my bag. He stopped, too, and waited, still as a photograph, a few steps above.

At this, I looked at the monk more closely. He was tall and gaunt, with sunken cheeks and deep-set eyes. His shaved skull showed the shadow of a few days' growth, his face recorded only a few lines and no furrows. He could have been thirty, he could have been fifty. Black tattoos adorned his hands and arms, which were bone-thin and strong: A snake curled across the back of his left hand; a five-point star, pierced by two arrows, hung in the smooth underside of his forearm; a band of small dots ringed each wrist like two narrow bracelets.

Something about those tattoos struck me as familiar. I looked again at the narrow face, looked into the quiet Burmese eyes. With a start, I realized he was my savior from the day before.

I smiled sheepishly. The monk grinned back in forgiveness, displaying a gap-toothed smile stained betel-nut red. Such smiles are common throughout Burma, the result of chewing the copper-colored nut, which is said to evoke a mild sense of euphoria.

"I walk Mandalay Hill every day," he explained, in answer to my unspoken question. "I knew you come one day. All visitors watch the sun go down from Mandalay Hill."

Despite the 1,729 steps, the half-mile walk to the top of Mandalay Hill is not difficult. A wood roof shading the open-air stairway keeps the stone path cool. The monk maintained an unhurried, even pace, taking the smaller steps two at a time. Every so often, without slowing, he would place a plug of betel in his mouth, chew a while, then spit the red juice off to the side.

We climbed in silence, past the souvenir vendors and palm readers stationed along the path, past old women resting on stone benches, chomping on fat, green cheroots. Midway up the hill, the monk halted at a large temple and motioned me inside. Inside were the so-called "Peshawar Relics," three bones of the Buddha.

Though the relics housed within may actually be real, they receive little attention from the Buddhist faithful. Much more venerated, for some reason, are the countless (and often suspect) Buddha hairs and Buddha teeth scattered throughout the world. Save for one small, grizzled man bowed low before the shrine, we were the only visitors to the temple.

Near the top of the hill we stopped once again, this time alongside a statue of woman kneeling before the Buddha, offering him her severed breasts. Legend holds that the woman was once a terrible ogress who, upon hearing the words of the Enlightened One, was so overwhelmed that she immediately changed her ways and devoted the rest of her life to following his teachings. As a symbol of her devotion, she sliced off her breasts.

The view from the top of Mandalay Hill extends far across the Irrawaddy plain, its flat surface and occasional jutting hill studded with the gold and white spires of pagodas and temples. In the waning light of late afternoon, they glittered like jewels laid across the throat of a beautiful woman. To the north stretched the rice paddies of the upper Irrawaddy. Spread out to the south was the golden city for which the hill is named, dominated by the enormous palace fortress. To the east, toward China, rose the purple outline of the Shan Plateau. To the west flowed the Irrawaddy River, its slow-moving waters framed by the gleaming hills opposite.

We sat down, my monk friend and I, to watch the sun set over the river. Since monks in Burma are forbidden to take anything directly from the hand of a woman, I placed my notebook and pen on the bench between us and asked him to write out his name for me. He did so, neatly filling the right-hand corner of a page in my journal with the charming bubbles that make up Burmese script. Opposite, I penned its phonetic translation: Oo Te Tee La.

We watched as the butter-dipped sun dropped low in the sky, watched as it slipped behind the thin clouds stretched across the horizon. Its angled rays painted the sky—first lavender, then peach—before melting into the pink waters of the Irrawaddy. As the last glow of day headed into night, the monk stood to go. He raised his hands palm-to-palm beneath his chin and bowed slightly. "Good-bye, Lo Ren," he said. "I hope you come again to Mandalay."

He turned and walked away, back toward the stairs we had so recently climbed together. I watched his angular form disappear from sight. Yes, I thought. I will come again to Mandalay.

Swiss Squeeze

PAMELA MICHAEL

Years ago, after watching a terrified tourist dangling from a speedboat-towed parasail slam into the facade of a beachfront hotel in Puerta Vallarta, I decided that were I ever to take up a dangerous sport, a country like Mexico would not be the place to do it. The same wisdom prompted me to turn down free scuba diving lessons in Egypt. Risking one's life for sport— no matter how exotic or beautiful the locale—had always seemed insane to me. And yet I think of myself as a fairly brave person and something of a fearless traveler. But then, chancing ambush to see Angkor Wat is quite a different proposition than hang gliding or bungee jumping just for "fun."

Not long ago, however, when I was invited to join an "outdoor adventure" tour to Switzerland that promised paragliding, river rafting and canyoning (sliding down waterfalls and belaying down cliffs, wearing a harness), so reassured was I by the Swiss reputation for precision and proficiency that I scarcely gave safety a moment's thought. A country that could produce more patent holders and Nobel Prize winners per capita than any nation on earth certainly could be counted on to muster guides I could entrust with my life.

My first few days in Switzerland only reinforced my admiration for Swiss competence, most visibly demonstrated by a remarkable transportation system of trains, ferries, funiculars, postal buses and mountain railways that rendered one of the most dramatic and daunting landscapes in the world—sixty percent mountains and twenty-five percent forest—as accessible as a city park. What's more, I could check my luggage from one hotel to another, so that when I arrived at my next destination my suitcase would already be in my room. This was the kind of "adventure travel" even an out-of-shape, middle-aged woman could learn to love. Switzerland, as eighteenth-century tourist Johann Goethe noted, is the perfect combination of the colossal and the well-ordered. And nowhere is this lovely Heidiland fusion of pine forests, alpine meadows, hillside villages and snow-covered peaks more sublimely realized than in the Engadine, the high valley of the En River, near the Italian border.

The Engadine is part of Switzerland's largest and most conservative canton, Graübunden, where women were given the right to vote only in 1971, where villages are connected by footpaths that date back 2,000 years to the Roman occupation. Indeed, the Bündner, as the residents of Graübunden are called, were the last people in the developed world to allow cars on their roads; they were banned until 1925. But even these stolid mountain people couldn't dam the eventual giddy flow of traffic to St. Moritz, the region's most famous resort town. Winter tourism to the Alps was virtually invented there by a hotelier in 1864 when he told his English summer guests that he'd pay their way home if they couldn't sit outside in their shirt sleeves in December. The mild climate that delighted the visitors of that long-ago December was even more appealing in the June of my visit. Wildflowers dazzled the eyes and nose. Flocks of fuchsia finches Eschered with yellow butterflies in the sparkling mountain sky. Cows, like four-legged vacationers, were arriving by train to summer in the high alpine pastures. In September, I was told, they'd be brought down again, cowbells clanging, their horns and necks bedecked with flower chains, to join a day of music and merrymaking in the villages.

Mountains are great shapers of character, it is said. And great stimuli for engineers, too—the challenge of living in such difficult terrain has goaded the Swiss to tackle almost every peak with a cog railway, tramway or tunnel. But it was the valleys and canyons that piqued my interest: the narrow gorges and wild cataracts of the Danube's scenic tributary, the En.

Our outfitters were something of an institution, it seemed. You'd see their colorful vans shuttling rafters along river roads, or gaggles of bicyclists with matching bikes and logoed helmets pedaling in slow motion up mountain passes. They had offices all over the country, many located in train stations. So practical, so convenient, so . . . Swiss.

Piling into the outfitters' van on the morning of our planned fourteen-mile rafting trip down the En, I had few misgivings despite the several Class V rapids we would face. "Without danger, the game grows cold," one of my traveling companions cracked as he threw himself into the back seat, rubbing his hands together in anticipation. I dismissed his comment as testosterone talk, the kind of bravado you might hear on ski slopes, rock faces or race tracks. I'd never quite understood the appeal of sports that could, and did, with regularity, kill or maim their participants. Whatever it takes to jam your poles into the snow and push off from the top of a ski jump, or to consign oneself to gravity and leap out of an airplane with what amounts to a floppy silk umbrella strapped to your back, I knew I didn't have.

Moderate risk, like river rafting—that I understood; a little fear heightened the experience and afforded a great sense of accomplishment at the end of the day. But really hazardous sports, of which the otherwise sensible Swiss seemed to enjoy quite a few, were a mystery to me.

Still, it was hard to feel in harm's way anywhere in Switzerland—everything worked so well. All the possibilities and contingencies of any situation seemed to have been taken into account. This assuredness that I was in good hands had settled into something approaching smugness on my part. I guess that's why I was taken so unawares by a rather unthinkable oversight on the part of the outfitters: They didn't have a wet suit large enough to fit me.

Now—it must be said—I am a big woman, at least the top half of me, which has become, in middle age, well . . . hefty. Though by some (almost cruel) twist of fate, I've retained the kind of strong, long Barbarella legs that thirteen years of ballet (and forty years of rock and roll) can forge. Consequently, I look rather as if I'd been put together from the body parts of two different people. But I'm not so large that there shouldn't be a wet suit large enough to fit me. There are lots of men much larger than I, and quite a few women.

There I stood in the river rafting equivalent of the tack room, in front of my traveling companions and a few strangers, surveying hanging racks of blue neoprene wet suits, all with two-foot high numbers scrawled on the back—sizes one to five. Ah yes, I'd be a five, by the looks of it, I thought. Oh great. Just like the bowling alley humiliations of my childhood, where the size—a big nine in my case—was printed right there on the back of your ugly shoe. Now I'm going to be crammed into a raft with a five on my back, surrounded by threes and fours and twos and maybe even a one.

"I'm not sure we have a wet suit to fit you," said the man handing out the gear, somewhat flustered.

"Do you have men's sizes?" I asked quietly, swallowing all pride.

"These are men's sizes."

"Oh." Tiny shiver.

"Why don't you try the five?" suggested our tour guide, ever optimistic.

I slunk off to the women's dressing room, a dank corner of the stone hut that housed the outfitters' extensive—but not extensive enough, as it turned out—gear. Other women were wiggling into their twos and threes, zipping them up the front with the tiniest of tugs, then skipping off like sprites while I struggled to squeeze my considerable belly into the clammy, sweat-soaked, foul-smelling suit so I could at least attempt to zip it up. Judging from the stench, there were no rest stops along the river—once this thing went on it stayed on until the end of the trip, no matter how long that happened to be. But mine wasn't going on in the first place. There was just too much of me bulging from the unzipped "V" in the front. No matter how elastic the suit, there was no way to zip all of me in.

My struggle was humiliating, so humiliating that I felt almost shrouded in a cloud of shame and frustration, cut off from the other women who were, no doubt, embarrassed to be watching me wrestle with my own body. The kindest of them broke through the cloud: "Want some help?"

Soon there were eight hands pressing, stuffing, cramming and tugging at flesh and zipper and blue neoprene. Four voices laughed and whooped and giggled, and one of them was mine. The mass of me was jollied up, up, up until it almost hit my chin. We got the zipper to about mid-sternum and had no choice but to let my now-enormous bosom, enlarged by folds of belly with no place else to go, swell up like some cartoon décolletage.

"I feel like I'm wearing a full-body Wonder Bra," I joked. Humor to the rescue.

A bright red life jacket added even more bulk but, blessedly, hid the mortifying number five. I could only hope that it would also hide the bulk of me the wet suit couldn't cover. I looked like a brightly colored Michelin woman in Ray Bans. I could barely turn sideways. Would I even be able to paddle in this get-up? And how could I possibly bear the embarrassed and amused smiles of my fit, young, limber companions as I waddled down to the water's edge? But there was a river to run, and this was the only body I had at my disposal to run it with; I swallowed my pride, took a deep breath (as deep as my neoprene-constrained lungs would allow) and lumbered out the door.

Risk comes in many forms—physical, emotional and even financial—but courage is a singular summoning of a part of ourselves and the universe that is as elusive as it is powerful. I was flush with newfound courage and determination as I joined the others on the rocky shore. The water was a milky blue-gray from ground-up rock known as glacial flour. Six of us—five "adventurers" and one real adventurer, our river guide, a blond dreadlocked Aussie nicknamed "Home Boy"—set off in a fourteen-foot raft and were quickly swirling through rapids with names like Meat Cleaver, Happy Snapper, Nipple Rock, Prussian Sling Shot and the aptly named Kotzmuhle, the Vomit Mill. Good river guides possess a necessary combination of river skills—strength, caution, the ability to "read" the water—and people skills, the leadership qualities needed to make greenhorn rafters Paddle Forward! High Side! and Hold On! at just the right times. Home Boy was a Crocodile Dundee/Lord Byron hybrid; he had the perfect blend of daring and sensitivity and we adventurers were soon throwing ourselves from one side of the raft to the other without hesitation on his command. The Michelin Woman was a little slow to resume her paddling position on the rim at times, but she scrambled gamely and with only half a thought of how she looked hoisting herself out of the bottom of the raft. During the lulls, she even found herself relaxing enough to take in the beauty of the En Valley.

In the quieter stretches of water, Home Boy pointed out some of the many streams that fed into the river from tantalizing, lushly-forested side canyons. Several of the gushing tributaries had heavy loads of iron that stained the rocks around the confluences a shocking red. We saw abandoned old *trinkhalles* along the shore, remnants of spas from another age. The region, in fact, has been a popular healing resort since the sixteenth century and still has several operating spas, including a palatial new one at Bad Scuol, located in a romantic village in the lower Engadine that calls its mineral water "the champagne of the Alps." We floated past the edge of the Swiss National Park, the oldest in Europe, established in 1914. In this oasis of wildness in the midst of a tamed and somewhat manicured country, it is possible to catch glimpses of marmots, red deer, ibex, lynx and chamois. Sadly, the protection of the park did not come in time for the last bear in Switzerland: It was shot within sight of the river in 1904.

Halfway through our run we came upon a raft from another outfit, "wrapped" around a large boulder in the middle of the river. The paying rafters sat shivering, despite their wet suits, on the rock-strewn banks while their guide struggled valiantly to free the raft, now swamped with water and barely above the surface. Home Boy parked us in an eddy along the shore and leapfrogged from boulder to boulder to reach the stricken craft. The two guides tried ropes, wedges, all kinds of ingenious—and previously employed, it was clear—techniques, some of them quite danger-ous, for at least an hour, in vain. The undercurrent had captured the raft and wasn't letting go. Disturbingly, we were in a particu-larly rugged and steep section of the gorge; it was clear there was no way to hike out from this spot on the river. But this was Switzerland, the Disneyland of nations, by *Gott,* where everything was under control, so Home Boy fished out his cell phone and called in a rescue team. We squeezed a couple of the colder refugees into our raft and pushed off, leaving the rest of the stranded rafters to await the rescue boat. Just down river we rounded a tight bend and—flash!—saw an eagle take wing in a spray of sunlit droplets of river water, a squirming fish grasped in its talons. An icy dribble splattered my upturned face as the eagle flew over our heads. It felt like a benediction.

I had become, for a moment, just another element in a shim-mering landscape of river, sky, tree, mountain, fish, bird. I let out an exultant whoop and fell back into the raft laughing, washed by waves of exhilaration, awe and gratitude. I had triumphed over my fears and been rewarded with this yodeling, soaring Alpine high. And I hadn't risked my life, really, just my pride. Small stakes, when you think about it.

Learning to Breathe

ALISON WRIGHT

The bus looked as if it had been split open like an overripe watermelon, its bloodied human contents tumbling from its sides. A big blond girl dangled awkwardly in mid-air, her body suspended between the two buses that had collided. A young dreadlocked backpacker lying by the side of the road looked up, a long metal rod piercing his cheek. Her arms extended in front of her, a Laotian woman with severe facial lacerations groped blindly. Stunned passengers stumbled along the road in a daze. Others panicked. It was mayhem in slow motion.

The air was heavy with dust and smelled thickly of burned rubber—brakes stretched beyond their limit. The bright midday sun was fierce. Birds screeched from the dense bamboo forests, echoing the anguished moans of the injured.

In the distance, voices called out repeatedly, "My God, someone do something! This woman is bleeding to death!" I silently prayed that someone would help her. I turned my head to look at my watch, saw the arm-length gashes. My arm looked like a shark had attacked it, my denim shirt soaked red. It was then that I realized that the woman they were talking about was me.

January 2: I had just left friends after celebrating the new millennium in Luang Prabang, Laos. As a travel photographer, I was working in Asia for a few months, and we had made arrangements to meet there and celebrate the New Year together.

That morning I got up before dawn and met with Jerry, a fellow photographer, to take pictures of the monks begging for alms in the streets. Suddenly realizing the time, I put my cameras away, not knowing that these would be the last photos I would take for a very long time. I raced to the bus station to catch the next bus to Vang Vieng, where I would continue traveling south on my own.

Despite years of traveling on local transportation, something about the bus made me uneasy. I changed my seat three times, not wanting to sit too close to the front. I remember feeling apologetic because the girl behind me was cold and wanted the window closed. I didn't like the look of the glass for some reason, and kept pushing the window open. Little did I know this would save my life.

We were about five hours into the journey when I put my Lonely Planet guidebook down. Having decided where to stay, I hoped to reach Vang Vieng in time to photograph during the golden sunset hour. Looking out the window, I noticed that every turn along the road was breathtaking—green undulating hills adorned with bamboo wisps, cavernous valleys and limestone caves. It was a treacherous drop from the roadside to the valley below.

I had shifted my gaze from the scenery when I saw the hefty blue bus coming around the corner toward us. Neither of the overloaded buses honked their horns in warning. I even saw the surprised faces of the other passengers and thought what a near miss it was.

Suddenly there was an explosive crash of crunching glass and metal, people shrieking. I was sandwiched between two seats that had crumpled into each other. Four seats behind the driver, I sat at the point of impact, next to the window. I felt my head bash the metal frame with a thud, my whole left side break, twist and snap. I was so blinded by brightness, I had to pause and ask myself if I had died.

My next thought was to grab my film, but I had no strength. I couldn't lift my body. We were enveloped in dense dust and smoke. People shouted "Fire!" and pushed their way down the aisle in a panic. It was then that I decided to forget my bag and, with an adrenaline rush, managed to pull myself off the bus through the front door. I fell immediately to the ground, then just sat quietly by the side of the road. Watching. Breathing in. Breathing out.

My back felt broken. There was a stifling tightness in my chest. I noticed blue paint running down my pants leg—from the force of the other bus. In between gasps I talked someone into going back on the bus for my film and money belt. The other passengers stopped a passing pickup truck and those of us most injured were loaded onto the open flat-bed. We bounced along for nearly an hour until we reached the small town of Kasi, which is really nothing more than a bus stop. I knew if my back were broken, I was really in trouble after that ride.

Throughout my ordeal, I meditated on my breath. I am convinced this is what saved me. I never lost consciousness, and I never went into deep shock. Never have I felt so aware. A practicing Buddhist, I was supposed to be heading to a three-week silent meditation retreat in India. Instead, this experience would turn out to be the practice of my life. For my life.

I was carried off of the truck by the driver and left on the floor of what I was told was a "health clinic." It was nothing but a bare cement room with cobwebs climbing the walls. Faint from the loss of blood, I laid my face against the dirt-covered floor. As I took in the surroundings, the severity of my situation hit me. "This is bad," I mumbled to myself, "This is really bad."

Local people stared at the few of us as we lay there. They had no idea what to do. No one spoke English. Finally, a boy in a white T-shirt poured alcohol on my open wound and stitched up my arm, without cleaning out the glass or gravel. No painkillers. I had no idea if the needle he used to sew me up was even clean. The agony was more than I would have thought possible to endure.

"We're in the Golden Triangle, for God's sake," I gasped, grabbing his collar. "Don't you have any of that opium you're all smoking up here?"

I was angry that I was going to die just because no one was able to get us out of there. It occurred to me that I could ask people to call the American Embassy until my dying breath, but if they didn't speak English, they simply wouldn't understand. Anyway, where would they get the embassy number? There were no phone books. I should have thought to write the number in my passport. This thought also hit me: My nationality doesn't matter, nor does my relative wealth. It doesn't matter how much money or how many credit cards I have. I'm stuck here just like everyone else.

I was told by another passenger that there were about twenty others injured, mostly foreigners, and that I was in the worst shape of anyone who had been moved to Kasi. At least two people had been killed immediately, including one of the drivers.

A young Dutch couple had been sitting behind me on the bus. Meia had broken her arm and had a concussion. I recognized her as the woman who had been precariously dangling between the two buses. Her boyfriend, Roel, who had just proposed to her the day before, was anxious but uninjured.

Roel was the only person who would listen to me. I kept repeating that I couldn't breathe and needed oxygen. When I could speak no more, I wrote notes. Apparently there are no phones in Kasi. Hours passed. No one got help. A woman from the German Embassy came by in a car. I still don't know why she didn't drive for help. She kept telling me that I couldn't breathe because I was afraid. This was frustrating, to say the least.

Finally, someone came in and said a helicopter was coming, then no, it couldn't fly at night. Opening my eyes, I was surprised to see that darkness had fallen.

That was when I knew I was going to die. It wasn't resignation, just an incredible clarity. My last scribbled note to Roel was, "I'm not going to make it through the night. I simply can't breathe anymore. Please call my brother, Andrew. His number is in my phone book. Tell him what happened to me."

Then I closed my eyes and let go. And here is the surprising thing: I let go of fear. An amazing calm came over me, a peace as I have never experienced before. I had total trust in the universe, an assurance that everything was exactly as it was meant to be. There was nothing left to do, nowhere left to go.

I didn't even feel sad as I thought of all those I love, of my new niece who I would never meet. Instead, I felt certain that I would see everyone again. I realized then that death ends life, not relationships. There was no need to be afraid. I was encompassed by the warm light of unconditional love, and I didn't feel alone. I felt I was being guided. It was the most profound experience of my life, one I will carry forever.

Someone took my hand. He introduced himself as Alan. A British national, he lived in Kasi, where he and his Laotian wife, Van, had started their own local relief organization. They also worked to detonate unexploded land mines and bombs left behind from the Vietnam war. More important, they had a truck. They told me that they would drive to Vientiane, the capital, and get an ambulance. Alan said later that as he held my hand and looked into my eyes, I mouthed, "There isn't time." It was now about 10 P.M. and I had been lying there for over eight hours. He warned me that he had been drinking all day because of the New Year. I laughed weakly. Did I have anything to lose at that point? Alan then kicked everyone into gear and they helped load me into the back of his truck.

Only six weeks earlier I'd had my palm read in Nepal. The fortune-teller predicted that I would be in a terrible accident. "That's an awful thing to tell me," I said, snapping my hand back possessively. It felt strange to be living out the premonition. I remembered that she also said I would be all right. That reassured me.

Roel and Meia accompanied me in the truck and, from the front seat, Roel occasionally called out my name so I wouldn't slip into unconsciousness. Alan did his best to avoid the numerous potholes. Bouncing on the hard corrugated metal in unbearable pain, I meditated on my breath the whole way.

"Bless your heart," Alan told me later. "We put you back there and you didn't say a word for five hours."

I focused on a sky full of stars. How beautiful they seemed. The feeling that I wasn't alone, that I was being watched over, stayed with me.

Another miracle: Alan was the only one in the area who had a radio telephone. He called the American Embassy.

"You had better meet us by the side of the road," I heard Alan tell them. "She's got serious spinal and lung injuries and she's not going to make it to Vientiane."

They were initially reluctant to meet us due to the recent guerilla warfare in the area. Thanks to Alan's persistence, however, they finally relented. Hours later, when Joseph De Maria and Michael Bakalar, representatives from the American Embassy, met us on the side of the road with an ambulance and a doctor, I was never so glad to hear an American accent in my life.

Because the medical facilities in Vientiane are extremely limited, the plan was to get me to Thailand, two hours south. At the border I was met by another ambulance and a paramedic at the Lao Friendship Bridge, who drove me yet another hour to the Aek Udon Hospital in Udon Thani, Thailand. By the time we arrived it was 3 A.M., over fourteen hours since the bus crash.

I was still unable to have painkillers, since they might have interfered with my breathing. At the hospital, Dr. Boonsam resutured my arm with over a hundred stitches, picking out some of the glass, gravel and metal that had not been removed. Looking at my x-rays, he told me in heavily accented English, "Another two hours, and I'm sure you wouldn't be here."

The doctor stopped counting the broken ribs after six. He confirmed that my lungs were punctured, as was my diaphragm. I had fractured teeth and huge contusions all down the left side of my body. I also had serious spinal injuries. My back, pelvis and coccyx were broken, my spleen ruptured. Most disturbing was that all my internal organs, including my heart, and even my bowels, had been torn out and smashed up into my left shoulder. What a visual. Listening to the litany as they prepped me for surgery I managed to say, "Please don't take out anything unless you really have to!"

Once the American Embassy contacted my family, word went out immediately. My brother and friends flew to my bedside. I had excellent care, and the nurses were all so sweet, except for the one who kept flipping my bed up and down at an alarming rate. Unable to speak through my respirator, I made the sign of the cross with my fingers whenever she came near me at bathing time.

Morphine-induced dreams haunted me for weeks. Images of the accident would jolt me out of my sleep with such force the bed would jump, sending the nurses into giggles. I dreamt of the window shattering, bloody bodies, waiting for the bus with friends. When it arrives I am so paralyzed with fear that I can't get on. They leave without me.

I appreciated the worldwide phone calls and e-mails from well-wishing friends. The cheerful switchboard operator always knew where to direct the long-distance phone calls, and even put a call through while I was on the operating table. I was especially grateful for the *pujas,* religious rituals for my well being, performed by the Dalai Lama and other Tibetan lamas I had met during my years of working on photo projects about Tibet. It was like coming back for my own funeral.

Nearly three weeks after the accident, Dr. Boonsam decided that I was strong enough to be transported to a hospital back home in San Francisco. He asked me if there was anything I wanted to do before I left Asia. I told him that I would really love to visit a temple and just sit for a while. I was surprised when he arranged for an ambulance and paramedic to take me to Wat Ba Baantad, a monastery famous for visits from the Thai Princess Sirindhorn. It was my first time outside the safe cocoon of my hospital room in fifteen days, and everything felt surreal. Using a cane, I managed to walk slowly to the altar on my own. Thai families made their offerings as the giant gold-leaf Buddha smiled down on us. As I sat meditating, trying to take in all that had happened, a young man invited me to have tea with the head monk. It was such a comfort just sitting with them.

The transition to health care in America was abrupt. The first thing the doctors wanted to do was cut off my Buddhist protection string that a lama had given me in Tibet. I had worn it around my neck during all my surgeries. I was adamant about keeping it on. It had gotten me this far, I reasoned. The ER doctors called me the miracle kid. I was told that even if the accident had happened in San Francisco they weren't sure if they could have saved me.

It's taken fifteen months of hard work and a few more surgeries to recover. On Halloween, which somehow seemed appropriate, I had an operation to rearrange my intestines and sew my stomach lining up with plastic mesh. I'm still picking out bits of glass and gravel that continue to work their way out of my arm, giving me terrible bouts of blood poisoning. After months of physical therapy, not only can I walk again, but I recently made a trip to the Arctic. I've gotten my lungs back and, except for some nasty scars and lingering pain, I should be able to climb mountains and scuba dive again.

People have told me what an awful way this was to bring in the millennium, and I'd have to agree. But it was also a rebirth. I've been given my life back, and every day now feels like a meaningful postscript. I found a strength within myself, both physically and spiritually, that I didn't know I had. It took a bus slamming into me to slow me down and for me to appreciate even more the preciousness of life and to share it fully with my friends and family. Every breath I take is a reminder.

From Somewhere to Nowhere

CARLA KING

I walk into the water at the pointy tip of India to let the Trinity flow around my ankles. Here is the confluence of the Arabian Sea, the Indian Ocean and the Bengal Sea. Here are the pilgrims, dabbling in the water and settling on the sand to contemplate and to pray to this great trinity—the creator, the protector, the destroyer. Brahma, Vishnu, Shiva. The father, the son, the holy ghost.

I chose to ride an obscure little back road from Madurai to Kannykumari, the end of India. It was a mistake. It is often a mistake to choose a back road in a country where even the main roads are back roads. It began well enough, lush and tropical, but changed abruptly to scrub and desolation. Sometime recently asphalt had been poured thinly onto the dry golden earth, resulting in a winding black ribbon, already crumbling at the edges into dust. The motorcycle chugged along undisturbed, but for me it was a lonely road, like the road to Big Bend through a dry Texas valley toward the Rio Grande, like the road through the Gobi with its windswept snakes of sand wending south to the Yellow River. It's along these roads that you start wondering if, by some fluke, you are the last living person in the world, and then suddenly someone appears walking from somewhere to nowhere. Where was she going, that woman in a bright green sari carrying the huge bundle of twigs on her head? And those two men with newly carved wooden pitchforks slung over their shoulders. Where might they use them, less than a day's walk away?

Another hour goes by and I'm still wondering where these people came from, where they were going. In four hours I stopped three times for other vehicles—two buses and a truck that kindly didn't force me off into the ditch. I stopped once for a herd of cows and once for a black spotted goat that trotted back and forth on the asphalt when he saw me. I might have dreamt my last forced halt to let fifty miniature burros pass by. They swarmed around the motorcycle, their long ears brushing my mirrors as they trotted toward an oasis with one tiny pond and a few spindly coconut trees. The scent of hot fur and manure lingered a moment, and then there was only dry heat in a landscape of sand and aloe and acacia and twisted little trees with flat tops, with a few withered leaves clinging to dry branches.

Still no village, still no petrol station—the source of a helpless underlying worry that remains with me. I follow the sun, setting its glare in my right eye, and continue down this southwest back road, as if I had any choice. I am twenty kilometers into the reserve tank, and my worry grows, but just when the engine begins to stutter from starvation, civilization appears.

I coast to the pump and welcome the shimmering rise of petrol fumes as the attendant splashes the first precious drops into the tank. It is hellaciously hot as I stand waiting for the tank to fill, and touts swarm me with promises of cheap hotels.

I ride away from them and toward the sea, to join the pilgrims. I sit on the beach and watch the horizon from this spot at the end of the world, the end of their world. The women are draped in all colors of silks and cottons, with scarves over their heads and gold discs in their nostrils, bangles on their wrists and barefoot, barefoot for all of their lives. A man in white and orange is having his photo taken to commemorate the moment, the highlight of his pilgrimage. He adjusts his white turban and strikes a severe pose, ankle deep in the sea. Beyond him a few people splash in the water, protected by the smooth brown rocks that break the waves. A sun-blackened hippie wrapped in gauzy Indian cotton perches on a larger rock, picking out a tune on an exotic small guitar. He smiles at me, then picks up the rhythm as two women wade into the water up to their thighs, their saris floating in the gently heaving tide like yellow and lavender seaweed. I press my bare feet into the sand and walk in after them, the brown cotton of my pants darkening with water.

The sea is warm and the salt stings my wounds. The sun is falling. The faces around me are quiet and smooth in meditation.

Many, sitting in groups on the sand, close their eyes. The bald heads of those who gave their hair at Tirupati are smeared with yellow ash. Nearly every forehead is dotted with red *kumkum* powder, swiped on by the priest during today's *darshan* blessing at the temple. They know why they are here, these pilgrims. They come in ragtag groups and huddle together around the buses in which they arrive. They make a tiny space for living, cooking and sleeping. They defecate onto the rocks at the sea wall at dawn and dusk. They go to the temple, worship, and they gather again, kneading dough for *chapati,* flattening them into discs, tossing them into a fire. Someone stirs a huge pot of watery yellow *dahl.* They are experiencing hardship, as is appropriate on a pilgrimage. The word "sacred" has its roots in the word "sacrifice," and they know the meaning of both. The road here is difficult, and they are poor, but they, at least, know what they are looking for. They, at least, know that they have found it, that they are fulfilling an agreement made from the beginnings of their many lives. And they know that this life is only one of many more to come.

I say that I am not a seeker, yet here I am in a country where seeking and finding is a natural part of life. Road signs warn, "Be Careful, Only One Life," but to Hindus, karma is a factor that tempers the fear of the end of this life, and if you die because you are driving like a maniac, well, it's out of your hands. It's your karma. But no matter, previous lives lived well promise reward in the next. You can speed up the process toward enlightenment by walking around mountains and deities and performing countless other rituals. Such rituals! They are lovely and frightful. I studied some; I copied the movements, the outward signs of worship, but always felt somewhat removed. I followed carefully in the bare footsteps of those walking through darkened hallways, down the stairs to the inner sanctum. I performed the *puja* ceremony to the temple gods along with the others, and received my *darshan* from the priest. Now I stand in the sea, my forehead swiped with red *kumkum* powder, too. A non-believer can pay respects, no? Even if she doesn't completely understand?

I am a child-person here, a foreigner, and they forgive me. Religion is not a game or entertainment for tourists, and I am a tourist, an unwilling spiritual tourist in this land of temples and sacred mountains. I have always made a little bit of fun of seekers, but India does something to you that creates a wondering. Within a week I found myself at Aurobindo ashram, and the next day I was meditating with the largest crystal in the world. There I found an energy that removed me from my physical self for just a little less than an hour. I floated for days on that energy, and I know that whatever shaped that clear pure stone is a spiritual force to be taken seriously, as serious as the velocity at which I hit the ground seven days ago.

I killed a dog. Does that shave some time from my process of enlightenment? I rub the seawater into my wounds and the salt stings good. The thick scabs that have formed on the tops of my wrists, my knees and my left shoulder are softening and beginning to bleed again. I remember the speedometer reading forty miles per hour but I have no memory of the impact, the tumbling. Only the sound of my helmet bouncing in my ears, and then blessed landing, unconsciousness, then water in my face. The dog was still screaming as they took my keys and put me in the van. They were Christian missionaries, Indians in fluttering white saris. They put me in the back, and I looked out the window. The dog lay still at the side of the road. It was a gray-black dog, an adult, healthy and vibrant, with short, shiny fur. There was no blood, but it lay panting heavily, its eyes open wide. I know I hit it square on, right in the middle. The moment before I hit it is frozen in my memory.

"Is the dog dead?" I asked the woman in the green sari who was performing Hindu blessings over my bloody knee.

"No," she said. "It is not yet dead." One of the missionaries started the motorcycle. Miraculously, it was undamaged.

"It will be dead soon?" I asked.

"Yes," she said. "It will soon be dead." She said one last prayer, and left me to the missionaries. No one paid attention to the dog.

I hated it for crossing the road like that, without looking. I thought it deserved to die, the stupid, hateful creature. And then I was sorry. So sorry. Weeks later I still fluctuate between the hate and the sorrow, and I remember, along with this confusion, the feeling of the blood, so warm at my knee, and then colder as it ran down my leg, soaking the white fabric of the fine cotton sari folded under me.

At the time I didn't even wonder at the fate of my knee, or of the rest of my trip. I was enfolded and unravelled, leaving my fate in hands other than my own. In India you look around and realize that since you've arrived there is no moment, not even one, that you can escape knowing where you are.

Now the sun sinks into the sea and I become a pilgrim. I am in India, with all its dirt and beauty. Each is balanced by the other; there is nothing that might be labeled bland. There is the boy with the twisted legs and the wide black eyes skittering on his hands along the sidewalk, silently begging. The woman, piebald with leprosy, glaring hate and spirit. The old crone with her hand sticking from a ragged silk sari, her toothless mouth croaking *"maw, maw."*

There is the glossy white cow that chews through banana peels and pomegranate husks. The girl child who supports her baby sister on a tiny, jutted hip. A line of *sadhus* in orange robes, sitting with their beards and their hollowed-out gourds along the swept-clean gates of an ashram. A stoned hippie argues with a rickshaw driver over a nickel's worth of taxi fare. Goats toss their heads as they rip through plastic bags at garbage piles, their yellow eyes glittering under the streetlight. An aluminum vat of green chili peppers pops and sizzles. Discarded banana leaves slimy with yellow curry lie in a pile by the curb.

It is difficult to look sometimes, but if you do, you begin to see past the dirt.

Geography of Dreams

CHRISTI PHILLIPS

I met you in an elevator. Moscow 1991, the first day of the August coup.

On the 20th floor of the Intourist Hotel, faces pressed against windows overlooking Red Square. Yours was one of them. Below, soldiers and tanks, the Kremlin surrounded, Moscow surrounded. A gray, solemn day of sullen drizzle, and a night that came on quickly, like a thunderclap.

I bumped into you, muttered *excuse me,* and turned away. When I stepped into the elevator, you were there.

Inside, just us. Outside, the tanks, the soldiers, the crowds that massed beneath Yeltsin's office at the Parliament building not far away. Outside, the streets rutted and torn by tank treads, blocked by barricades.

Inside, just us, alone.

I met you in an elevator. We were going down.

The hotel restaurant was a good place to hide out, as there was nowhere else to go. A jazz quartet played on a small stage; rain on the windows added a steady percussion. No champagne or vodka, so we drank cognac. No food except beefsteak, which arrived hours later, barely edible.

Son of an Argentine Communist, schooled in Russia, you were directing your first film in Tbilisi. You'd come to Moscow to buy film ends, black market stock sold by Russian cinematographers. Guerrilla filmmaking, you said. No way back to Tbilisi now.

No way back now.

Talking in the dark. You could speak five languages, could say "I love you" in six. A lone candle flickered light on the most compelling face I'd seen since coming to Moscow, on long black hair that fell past your shoulders and into eyes I recalled from Picasso's early paintings. Long-legged, trim, a boy's body, but you were already past thirty then. You wore faded jeans and an old blue sweater over a threadbare cotton shirt: the bohemian suit of an artist.

I wanted to kiss you.

Right away, I wanted to kiss you.

I never told you that.

Films had also brought me to Moscow, by way of a writing assignment from a Russian film studio. It was offered at a time when I imagined that I would never fall in love again, so Moscow seemed as good a place to be as any other.

How long will you be here? you asked.

Three more months. Unless the coup succeeds.

Of course. Only three months and then you fly away?

Yes. I fly away.

We said goodbye first. Said goodbye before we kissed, as if we would never see each other again. Who could be sure?

It never ended, that kiss. Hours in the doorway of my hotel room. Then we moved back inside and you softly shut the door behind you.

If I could kiss you now I would kiss you just as we kissed then. Even if it meant being transported back to that place: the low gray sky, rutted streets, soldiers marching, scent of hysteria in the air.

In a country of want, desire has no end.

The third night of the coup, you bribed a waiter at the Hotel Peking and he led us to the last unoccupied table in the restaurant. The coup leaders had fled only hours before, and every hoarded bottle of vodka in Moscow was emptied in the first post-Communist blow-out. All around us, people laughed maniacally. Drunk couples staggered past, swaying and slipping as they held each other up.

The night before, you'd been picked up by the militia for violating the curfew. You smiled and shrugged it off: *I'm from Buenos Aires. I grew up with tanks and soldiers.*

Your grandfather and uncle were two of Argentina's "disappeared," swallowed up in Peron's prisons and never seen again.

Your grandmother wore black for the rest of her life. She had dreams in which she would find them in exotic places: tropical jungles, endless deserts, places that you were sure she had never been or even read about. Every night she set places at the table for the men she could not feed; you, your sister, and your parents ate dinner while looking at the two empty chairs. *It was very strange, like living with ghosts.*

Nothing mattered then but that I wanted you.

In my hotel room high above Red Square, we listened to Schubert and the rain. Dark room, tiny shaft of light from the open bathroom door. Hours not speaking. Growing closer through sensation, without words, in a way there were no words for.

You went back to Tbilisi. I heard your voice faintly crackling through miles of static-filled telephone lines. You told me stories of guerrilla filmmaking, of impending civil war. President Gamsakhurdia had become a dictator, was holed up in his palace only two blocks from your flat. Illiterate men from the Georgian mountains were bused in to guard him, given vodka and guns and marched around the palace periphery. Crowds gathered nightly, shouted freedom slogans and threw stones. Brutish militia kept order with brutish methods.

Because of my long hair, they're always stopping me.

Leave. Don't make your film there.

I have no choice.

The year before you'd been invited to Tbilisi, had taken your guitar. Hazy memories of a night of drinking and singing.

In Georgia, there is a song for everything, and you and your guitar played them all. The night of many toasts, you called it, but before you passed out you told your hosts about the film you wanted to make. The next morning a producer rousted you from under the table where you slept and said he'd finance your film, as long as you made it in Georgia.

I've seen the militia pull men out of cars at gunpoint for nothing. . . . don't worry, I know how to deal with it.

I worry.

What would they want with me, anyway? I'm just a guy with a camera.

That's the most dangerous kind of guy.

I have a photograph of you. You lie on your side on my hotel room bed, elbow crooked, facing me. Arabesques of smoke trail upward from the cigarette in your hand. Your face, I realize, is not just from Picasso's paintings, it's Picasso's own face. An elongated oval, exaggerated eyes, thick brows, strong nose. Skin the color of café au lait, paled by too many years in northern climes far from home. Dark stubble on your cheeks and chin and upper lip that reappears in less than a day. Hair so black it's prismatic.

All your features considered this way make an interesting face, not a beautiful one. That's what you would say, *not beautiful.* Yet when I first saw you my breath left my body.

In the photo you stare straight at me, as if you knew that later I would look at you and you wanted to reply, *I am looking at you.* I imagine that I can hear your voice.

If we want to be together, what will stop us? The world is not such a big place, no?

We did what lovers do in times of war or peace: walked through Moscow's quiet Sunday streets, hands clasped, the salt-water taste of your skin on my lips; kissed in pale birch forests turned golden by the autumn sun. A dark hotel room, a tiny shaft of light, we memorized each other slowly, endlessly.

Muy linda, you said. We were not afraid to look at each other. It had been like that from the beginning, from the moment you first raised your eyes to mine. Your lightly callused fingertips brushed my cheek, my throat. *Come here, I want to kiss you.* But I wanted to look at you for a moment longer. I wanted to make everything last. I wanted to forget that I was leaving soon.

You sat down on my bed and pulled me closer. We were happy but we did not smile, there was so little time for laughter. What happened so easily, almost carelessly, had surprised us both. Now we talked about visas and airfares. You had taught me how to say "I love you" in six languages.

You must go back to Tbilisi but would return to Moscow in time to take me to the airport. After that, there would be only letters and late-night phone calls before we saw each other again.

Don't be sad. The world is not such a big place, no?

No, it's not so big, I said, but I did not believe it.

Your voice and static traveled the miles between Tbilisi and Moscow. Stories of nightly skirmishes, people wounded and killed. Militia drunk on fear and power. One night you were engulfed by a crowd storming the palace. A soldier's bullet, and the man next to you fell at your feet.

Get out now, before it's too late.

But it was already too late. The civil war broke out in full fury, and Gamsakhurdia won the first round. The telephone lines were cut off, the borders closed. Hundreds were arrested, wounded, killed.

I waited for days. Waited in my hotel room high above Red Square for the phone to ring again. I watched the sun rise over the Moskva River. I watched the moon rise over the Moskva River. I waited until I could no longer wait.

Where did they take you? A shivering cell where you nursed your shattered fingers, bruises, blood?

Each night I look for you in a world I've never seen before, a geography of dreams. A desolate border town where the only common language is the unspoken word. A dense jungle in the shade of crumbling temples built by a race that vanished centuries ago. An indolent river that flows to a secret sea, where the bones of the drowned float to the surface and shimmer like stars.

When ancient cartographers reached the end of the known world, they wrote, *Beyond this there be dragons.* That is where I found you: alone, on an empty plateau at dusk. You stood still, your guitar at your side.

I wanted you to speak.

I wanted to hear you say that they did not leave you broken, bloodied, hurt. I wanted you to tell me it was over quickly, that you did not suffer, but you had no words of comfort.

There is a song for the disappeared, you said, *and it sounds like silence.*

Maddening Madagascar

LISA ALPINE

The prostitutes thought our son Galen was a real gentleman. In fact, maybe the only gentleman (besides his father), in the crowd dining *al fresco* in front of the Hotel du France in Antananarivo.

It was our first night in the capital of Madagascar after a flight from Nairobi. At the suggestion of a fellow traveler, we had added this stop to a safari trip in Kenya. It took a while for us to realize that the well-heeled, denim-clad young girls milling around us in the restaurant were plying their trade. Packs of hungry-eyed children clustered behind the iron fence separating the patio from the sidewalk. The girls passed food and money to the youngsters— family members waiting to be fed. While the girls waited for men to consign their services, they bounced our blond, blue-eyed three-year-old on their knees. Cutest Westerner they'd ever seen.

That night, when we bedded down in our room, haunting sounds of creaking springs and frequent groans seeped through the walls. Sleep eluded us as deep male grunts confirmed our suspicions that this hotel was not on the *Relais et Chateaux* route.

At six the following morning, we shuffled off to the train station and set out to explore the mysteries of Madagascar in a nineteenth-century "iron horse." Late in the day we disembarked at Perinet, on the edge of a lemur preserve, and checked into a dilapidated hotel next to the train station.

One of the wonders that lured us to Madagascar was its prolific and unique flora and fauna. This red-earth island, 250 miles off the coast of East Africa, is the place to find grotesquely shaped Baobab trees, mysterious underwater coelacanths (fish once thought to be extinct) and mouse lemurs, the smallest primates in the world.

We worked hard to see nature's wonders. A guide led us into the rainforest and we searched for *indri-indri,* one of thirty-three lemur species found only in Madagascar. Treading for miles beneath the dense canopy, we craned our necks looking for this endangered and elusive lemur, which sleeps eighteen hours a day. Finally, several *indri-indri* stirred the canopy a hundred feet overhead, and we were treated to a brief glimpse of furry behinds.

The next morning my husband again felt the lure of the lemur and took off with the guide into the yawning green. Galen and I chose to explore a local village. We found a town near the train tracks and were soon surrounded by a swarm of jaundiced children with bloated stomachs and brittle hair. Sewage trickled down the gullies beside the dirt track that wound through town. I held onto my son, who wanted to pass out candy. How do you pass out twenty-five pieces of candy to hundreds of children?

My husband found me crying at the hotel. It had broken my heart to see children in such a hopeless situation while my robust son, wrapped protectively in my arms, reached out to them, wanting to share his candy stash.

That night we boarded a train for a ten-hour ride to Tamatave, a town under martial law. Rumors spread through the train that just the day before, the Malagasy (people native to Madagascar) had rioted against Hindu residents, exiling hundreds. To add to our discomfort, torrential sheets of rain pounded on the steamy windows. There was no food, water, electricity or ventilation. The windows were rusted shut. Only the lightning bolts illuminated the train interior at night.

Desperate for a breath of fresh air, I disembarked at one stop by myself and stood in the pouring rain, refusing to get back on. My husband grabbed my arm and yanked me onto the train as it began to move away from the platform.

In Tamatave, we stayed in another whorehouse. It seemed all the "decent" hotels were bordellos. We were beginning to wonder where the other tourists were. By the end of the two-week trip we had encountered only a handful: two French expats from the nearby island of Réunion and three Russian scientists on leave from their expedition boat. After the French colonists left

Madagascar in 1960, the country became Marxist and closed its doors to Westerners. The doors were beginning to creak open again; it seemed we were among the first tourists allowed in.

As we left Tamatave, it was hard to ignore all the broken shop windows from the rioting of the day before. We were flying from civilized madness to Isle Saint Marie, a coconut-strewn haven cloaked in romantic history, the retirement spot for legendary pirates.

We boarded the small plane, thinking it was our escape to a real vacation. We headed into a tormented sky. The wind god played ping-pong with our aircraft. I crossed myself. I'm not Catholic, but it beat biting off my nails. Touch down we did, though, right before I threw up. Nobody got off the plane but us, yet people were pushing to get on. We soon learned that a cyclone was coming. Cyclones are very noisy. And wet. And they last several days. We were stuck there for four days, staring at the downpour with our ears plugged. Not a shred of blue sky. At night we slept under the bed on the concrete floor, afraid the roof would blow off. On a positive note, we were served an unlimited amount of lobster for lunch and dinner.

We finally got off Isle Sainte Marie, but things did not improve. One of our worst days involved a twelve-hour ride sitting on leaky gasoline cans in one-hundred-degree heat, bouncing over a pot-holed dirt road. My husband suffered the most, his skin carpeted with a red rash from eating too much lobster.

The driver dropped us off in Ambanja, a town with not a single motorized vehicle in sight. The streets were a swirl of livestock, saronged women, wary-eyed men and throngs of children. It was too hot to be inside at night. Charcoal braziers smoked in front of huts. Our lodging was a dive, but they had beer.

Beer was our savior. We sat on rickety chairs in the middle of the road, swigging Three Horses, the local beer, and watching Galen cavort with a baby goat. I felt happy, ecstatic even. Perhaps this remote pageant of humanity milling before us swathed in bright colors, dark skin glowing from the firelight, was worth the horrendous ride.

The beer not only went to my head, it also went to my bladder. I walked giddily to the outhouse and entered the pitch dark. I heard a scurrying noise and turned on my flashlight. Two fat rats eyed my descending bare bottom. I felt too sick to even scream.

The mosquitoes in Ambanja are chloriquine-resistant and we couldn't give Galen the other antimalarial drug, because it is too strong for children (and probably adults). If one of the several hundred constantly hovering bugs bit Galen, he had a high probability of getting malaria. We were on mosquito (and rat) alert all night. Buzz, swat. Buzz, swat. Buzz, swat.

The next morning, we waited with others at an inlet for a boat to Hell-Ville, on the island of Nosy Be, Madagascar's only beach resort. The town's name made me uneasy. Why was it named after the Devil's abode? It was the only English town name we had encountered. I wondered what the Malagasy names meant. Tamatave: *town of broken glass?* Ambanja: *land of ass-biting rats?* A white-washed steamer pulled up after the requisite half-day delay. The ocean was as smooth as glass. Dolphins broke the placid emerald surface. A Chinese family offered us sticky buns and tea. In Chinese-accented French, they told me how the sister boat of the one we were on had sunk a month before. They all turned and pointed. There she was sticking her nose up out of the water. "Everybody died," they said. "Too many passengers for old boat. Like today . . . too many." They seemed calm. Why should I worry? They weren't. I counted heads and clenched my jaw with every tilt of the boat.

Finally, Nosy Be appeared on the horizon and we were still afloat. We docked in Hell-Ville and checked into a Holiday Inn, complete with clean towels, French cuisine and movies at night. Ironically, the town with the most foreboding name turned out to be normal, and I was bored. After all we'd seen and done, it just seemed so dull.

Some days in Madagascar I was on cruise control just so I wouldn't go out of my mind. At those times I'd write murder mysteries in my head, pray for a cold beer, clean my fingernails. We came to appreciate the simple pleasures only after we'd had our vacation illusions pounded out of us. Our last night, a scraggly troupe of Chinese acrobats were in town, and for thirty cents we watched them balance on top of twenty chairs and do pretzel-shaped contortions.

Would I go back? Yes, but I'd leave my son at home and expect the unexpected. Galen, if he could remember, would probably tell a whole different story, one filled with odd wonders—bug wings the size of his hand, kid goats frolicking with him on the street and plane rides reminiscent of Mr. Toad's Wild Ride at Disneyland. I'd have a hard time keeping him from coming along.

On Pleasures Oral

LINDA WATANABE MCFERRIN

Lawrence and I had sampled only a small part of Venice when Monica arrived. Disembarking at the Piazza San Marco, we crossed it, noting the Duomo's landmark rotunda, the rows of apostles draped in scaffold and net. We checked into our hotel, the Panada, at five o'clock and had dinner at ten—a very light supper at the Pescatore Conte.

The next morning dawn awakened us, weaseling its way in through the casements, creeping down draperies, columning them in substance. The scent of baking bread followed the light, then sound—the clatter of pots and pans, of children's voices rising from the street below.

When Monica disembarked, we were seated at a sidewalk cafe on the perimeter of the Piazza San Marco. Across the wide, noon-bright circle of the piazza, she progressed, a scintillating clove-brown figure, an exotic and imperious Cleopatra clad in a saffron blouse and billowing peasant skirt, preceded by a porter carting her enormous black suitcase and a few smaller bags. Her head was uncovered, scarved only in the straight black fall of her hair. She seemed made for the heat. Her Italian movie-star carriage had the usual grand and eye-stopping effect. Pigeons scattered. Heads turned. Men's hands reached involuntarily out toward her as she passed, thumbs and forefingers kissing in empty pinches that would never be consummated.

At that moment, I realized that I loved Monica in the same way that I loved my Barbie dolls as a child, with the passionate attachment one feels toward an ideal shimmering on the distant never-to-be-attained horizon. Men also had this feeling for her.

Lawrence and I pushed back our chairs, threw our napkins down next to our plates and advanced toward her with the well-choreographed precision of two chorus line extras supporting the principal dancer.

She rewarded us with a white flash of smile.

"*Ciao*," she sang out to us. "When did you get here?"

"Last night," we answered in unison.

"Don't you love it?" Monica crooned, echoing the plump pigeons that cooed, pecked and preened around our ankles and feet, their feathered bodies pressing carelessly up against us.

"More so, now because you are here," we responded.

"Well, I *have* to get rid of this luggage," she confided with well-practiced urgency. "Then, I will show you *my* Venice."

I've always felt very small next to Monica, small and child-like, like a pawn. My adoration only increases when I see the impact she has on everyone else. On her ample bosom, Lawrence's head had found a place to come, metaphorically, to rest. At least, I hoped it was metaphorical. I watched the two walk, arm-in-arm, ahead of me while I dawdled on bridges and the chipped, gap-toothed buildings leaned toward us, leering like doddering courtiers drunk with the sunlight.

"Where did you eat last night?" Monica asked as we walked past a series of port-side cafes on the Canale Della Giudeca.

"At the Pascatori Conte," Lawrence replied.

"Hmmm," she said thoughtfully, as if trying it out in her mind. "I've never eaten there." She paused for a moment considering this. "Well, tonight," she said with a long, slow smile "we will dine at the Bai Barbacani. It is better even than that one, Au Pied de Cochon, in Paris, remember? You will love it. I'll introduce you to Aldo, the owner. I wonder if he will remember me?"

There was no doubt in my mind about this.

We expected other friends to join us in the afternoon, but they arrived exhausted and ill. Dinner for them was out of the question.

Night had pitched its black tent over the city. Monica, in her sunflower-yellow dress, gleamed like a beacon beneath the lanterns that lined the narrow alleyways near the canal. On the marled stone walls that rose from the shadows on the opposite bank, small windows opened like the tiny doors in an advent calendar, torchlit, adventures seeming to smolder within their confines. The entrance to the Bai Barbacani was behind one of these windows.

We crossed a narrow bridge to Calle del Paradiso, on the other side of the canal. At the portals of the Bai Barbacani we were greeted by a slender, tuxedoed waiter who escorted us into the cavelike interior to a round white-clothed table where the candlelight danced, sylphlike, over crystal, china and silver.

Light flooded over Monica's shoulders, pooling gracefully at the juncture of her breasts. Her eyelashes cast shadows on the rise of her cheeks. Lawrence's hair glinted fiery.

Our waiter seemed adequate, but Monica was still restless, her eyes on a tall broad-shouldered man impeccably dressed in a double-breasted blue jacket cut to enhance a narrow waist.

He was making his way across the room, stopping at each of the tables and chatting with guests. His progress was arrested at the table next to ours, for he seemed to have found among these diners several dear friends.

"Aldo?" I asked.

"No," said Monica.

"Aldo is not here," she added with just a *soupçon* of petulance. I noticed that the slightest of pouts had settled upon her carnation-red lips. The restaurant seemed to have changed, to have been rearranged. Gone were the dusty bottles of homemade *fragolino* that Monica had raved about. The broad-shouldered man was laughing, leaning into the table right next to us, ignoring our table completely. He summoned a waiter who disappeared into the back of the restaurant and returned with what must have been a very special bottle of wine. It was uncorked with great ritual. The diner who sampled it nodded his head furiously. The broad-shouldered man squeezed his arm and moved on to us. His dark hair was thin and cut very short. He had eagle-like features.

"Welcome to the Bai Barbacani," he said, in musically accented English.

"Where's Aldo?" Monica demanded in response.

"He is gone," said our host.

Monica let him know that Aldo was missed.

"I was here before Aldo," the man replied simply. "I went away and now I am back. Aldo is gone."

He said this with the finality of a man who is used to fitting his confreres with shoes of cement.

"I don't believe you," Monica whispered tauntingly. "I think you have Aldo locked up in the basement."

"So," the man said, looking down at Monica, noticing appreciatively the way the darkness gathered at the top of her breasts like a pendant of jet and, sliding between them, disappeared into the soft yellow fabric of her bodice.

He looked up at us and smiled.

Monica told the man that Aldo had promised her certain secrets—"secret recipes"—when she returned, and she wasn't pleased to find him no longer there. Our new host was given to understand that she liked him less.

He asked her, "You don't like me as much?"

Monica shrugged and smiled. "I miss Aldo," she said.

It was a challenge, a gauntlet thrown down. Then it began—the wooing. Perhaps it was the candlelight that bathed everything in a kind of fairy-tale beauty, perhaps it was the desire to best the chivalrous Aldo or maybe it was the Circean net that Monica carried for occasions like this one. Whatever the cause, though the waiter returned and was very solicitous, the man could not seem to stay away from our table.

"Come, come back to the kitchen with me. I can show you how to stir the risotto," he said archly.

We had visions of Monica being abducted into the back, into the restaurant's nether regions, into the basement where Aldo was most certainly buried.

Monica laughed. "Maybe," she said. "Maybe later."

For an appetizer Monica ordered a bowl full of mussels, and our host nearly swallowed his tongue. Piled high on their perfect white china bowl each glistening shell held the tiny mollusk that has been compared to that most delicate part of a woman's anatomy. Pry open the shell, shut tight as virgin's thighs, and you feast on the sweet mound of flesh in its own fragrant liquor. Dress them with wine or eat them undressed—either way, to consume them is heaven.

Paulo (by this time we knew his name) leaned over Monica's shoulder and asked, not so innocently, if she'd like him to put a little lemon on them. Monica said "yes," so he called over the waiter who arrived with the proper tools—a silver plate holding a gauze-wrapped half-lemon and a small silver spoon. Paulo expertly disrobed the lemon and took firm hold of the spoon. He very aggressively screwed his small spoon into the lemon, dribbling its juices all over Monica's mussels. Monica watched him. He continued to screw away, eyes upon hers, really building up a sweat in the process. It seemed to go on forever. I was amazed. I'm sure none of us thought there could be that much juice in a single lemon. But Paulo was determined to lemon-up the mussels to Monica's satisfaction or knock himself out in trying. It was pathetic.

"Monica," I wanted to plead, "make him stop."

As if reading our minds, Monica finally said, "That's enough."

"Thank you," she purred demurely. Imaginary handkerchiefs went to three foreheads—Lawrence's, Paulo's and mine.

I had ordered sweet and sour sardines for an appetizer. I do not want to speculate upon their metaphorical value. Lawrence had ordered mussels as well, but all he got were a few cursory twists of lemon from the waiter.

Monica consumed her mussels with incredible gusto and even offered a few to me, though she knows that I'm allergic to shellfish. It's an allergy I developed recently and one that I never manage to recollect without a puritanical pang.

The appetizers had nearly exhausted us. I wasn't sure we were ready to deal with our entrees. To calm my nerves, I ordered risotto—a sweet pearly mixture, perfectly flavored, designed to comfort the taker. Lawrence had scampi—meaty pink prawns that he separated from their wafer-thin jackets of exoskeleton with fingers perfumed in lemon water.

Monica ordered gnocchi, a regional favorite. Satiny black pillows colored with cuttlefish ink and bathed in a fragrant salmon-red sauce—before us the simple potato dumplings lay, transformed into something incredibly sexy.

"Round two," I thought. "Victoria's Secret. Frederick's of Hollywood."

Paulo appeared, again, along with the entrees.

"This is the perfect choice for you," he said to Monica, his hand, braceleted at the wrist, gesturing toward her plate.

"I love those colors," giggled Monica.

"Come to the kitchen with me," Paulo challenged with a canine grin. "I will show you how it is done."

Monica laughed, "I'll bet," she said, and bit into one of the little black pillows. Her sharp teeth cut a tiny half-moon out of one side. I'd swear Paulo was salivating.

"Do you know," he asked, warming to the subject of food as he watched Monica eat, "do you know how I like to eat spaghetti?"

"No, how?" asked Monica.

"I float a wooden bowl of spaghetti in my swimming pool." His large hands placed an imaginary bowl upon the cobalt-blue waters shimmering in front of him.

"Then I float up to it."

We could now picture him in swim trunks, approaching the spaghetti that bobbed in its big wooden bowl on the water's flickering surface.

"Then, I suck the spaghetti slowly out of the bowl," he said, looking down at Monica. He was grinning from ear to ear.

"Oh, that sounds wonderful," Monica responded, placing her napkin beside her plate and gazing up into his dark brown eyes.

"You could try it," he said, raising an eyebrow.

"Do you know what my favorite food is?" Monica countered. "It is *mascarpone* cheese. Do you know how to make *mascarpone?*"

"Yes," said Paulo. "This cheese takes a long time."

"It does," agreed Monica. "I make fabulous *mascarpone*. I can teach you to make it my way."

"I would love to make *mascarpone* with you," said Paulo formally. I half expected him to salute.

"*La vie est belle,*" Monica laughed.

"*Toujours l'amour,*" Paulo chimed back.

The clichés began flying back and forth like shuttlecocks. Paulo would not leave our table. He catered to us to the point of neglect of the rest of his clientele. Diners ordered desserts and after-dinner drinks. He ignored them. Regulars paid bills and left the restaurant. He ignored them.

We struggled through apple strudels and tortes and polished things off with homemade *fragolino,* a strawberry liqueur more fragrant, Monica declared, than Aldo's.

"This is my *fragolino,*" Paulo said with great pride.

It was like perfume, really, a dark beautiful perfume. We chuckled and whispered that he probably had Aldo locked up in the basement making the stuff. Hours had passed. Candles had burned down to mere stumps. All of the other diners were gone.

"Will you come again, tomorrow night?" Paulo asked Monica, leaning over her chair, his mouth close to her ear.

"No," Monica said, turning her face to his, her nose nearly touching the sharp beak that was his. "No, but I'm here every year."

"Well," he said, as she rose from the table, "you must come again next year."

He took Monica's arm and escorted her gallantly back to the restaurant's threshold. "I will give you the secret then, to the *fragolino,*" Paulo said solemnly exchanging cards with Monica, promising her the recipe "next year," if she came, just as Aldo once had.

Lawrence and I knew better, of course. We had seen this happen before. We knew that the meal most longed for is the meal not yet eaten. We knew that Paulo's appetite had been aroused. And we knew, for certain, that sometime—long before the promised next year—there'd be a knock on Monica's door, and there he would be—the man with a hunger for *mascarpone.*

Progressive Supper

JACQUELINE HARMON BUTLER

Ernest Hemingway called Paris a "movable feast," and I have always agreed with him. On my last night in Paris, I decided to have my own movable feast—a progressive supper, with each course in a different restaurant. I wanted the restaurants to be within walking distance from one another, the last one near my hotel in the 6th arrondissement.

I was feeling a bit lonely and disappointed that I hadn't fallen in love with anyone this trip. I had already told my friends back home that this time I would meet that "special someone" while in Paris. Now, here I was, my last night in town, and still alone.

It was a perfect late summer evening. The sun set with an explosion of orange, pink and violet as I sat sipping my Kir Royale at the Café d'Flore. I took a leisurely stroll through the old neighborhood, pausing now and then to window-shop. I wandered across the Pont des Beaux-Arts and over to Les Halles and the restaurant Au Pied de Cochon.

As the maitre d' escorted me to a choice table on the terrace, I stole furtive glances around the room, hoping there would be a single man within easy flirting range. Alas, there seemed to be only couples or groups of women nearby. My waiter, though cute, was far too young. I sighed and decided a little Champagne and oysters would cheer me up considerably. Nor could I resist a bowl of delicious onion soup, washed down with a cool glass of Provençal rosé. Yes, I thought, I'm feeling much better.

I meandered a few blocks to L'Escargot Montorgueil for a few escargots. They were plump little darlings, swimming in garlic and butter and dusted all over with chopped parsley. I chose a wonderful old Burgundy red to accessorize the dish. Yummmmm, I thought, what a splendid idea. Suddenly, over the rim of my wine glass, I noticed an attractive Frenchman looking my way. Ooh la la, I thought. Things are looking up. Then he smiled at me and I felt I would faint. When he got up from his table, I was certain he was coming over to meet me but he walked right by. With a sinking heart, I watched as he embraced a glamorous blonde. My beautiful escargots, so delicious a moment ago, seemed to coagulate on the plate. I paid my bill and left the restaurant without even looking at the handsome Frenchman and his friend chatting cozily in a corner of the bar.

My mood was somewhat dejected as I crossed the Pont Marie to the Ile St. Louis. Gliding along the Seine below was a grand sightseeing boat, a Bateaux Mouche, its lights blazing against the old buildings. The decks were filled with happy couples laughing and pointing out the sights to each other. Romantic music came floating up to me and I could see couples dancing on the upper deck. Looking down along the quai I saw pairs and pairs of lovers strolling hand in hand. Others were sitting close together along the water's edge, locked in tight and feverish embraces.

Somehow I didn't feel hungry anymore. My plans to go to L'Orangerie for a leg of lamb and a rich Bordeaux no longer seemed interesting. By now I was feeling absolutely wretched and sorry for myself, so I decided to wander back toward the hotel.

The Pont Neuf looked beautiful with lights reflecting off the stone facade. I had photographed the bridge earlier in the day and decided to capture a few night images. Working took my mind off my loneliness and the lighting was perfect. I photographed the bridge from one side to the other and then from the top and from the bottom. Wanting to get some long shots, I walked over to the Pont des Beaux-Arts. Looking through the view finder I caught my breath. The wide-angle lens had captured the entire bridge shining golden in the night light, with the sparkling Seine below.

Ah, Paris, I sighed, how could any city be more lovely than you? I stood there, body tingling and heart swelling. Tears came to my eyes and I forgot all about my loneliness and depression. Then, as if on cue, a deep, sensuous voice said, *"Bon soir, Mademoiselle."* I turned around to gaze into a gorgeous pair of laughing, chocolate-brown eyes.

Chinese Like Me

JENNIFER LEO

for the first time in my life I was attracted to
Asian men. It happened on my first trip overseas, to be exact—in
Hong Kong, thirty-four hours before Great Britain ceremoniously
handed its Crown Colony back to China. Journalists were all over
the island, schedules in hand, looking for anything newsworthy.
The world was watching, waiting for change.

I was in the press lobby on the 26th floor of the Wanchai
Towers, 7,000 miles away from home in San Francisco. My friend
Alison was somewhere down the hall trying to finagle last-minute
press credentials, and I sat by the front desk wide-eyed and overwhelmed, while reporters from around the globe rushed by to
check in.

I've been attracted to men of all ages, from five years younger
than I to twenty years older. I've run my fingers through the locks
of brown hair, blond hair, red hair, black hair—and over the heads
of some men with not much hair at all. I've loved Caucasian men,

admired African-American men, fantasized about Latino men, but never once have I seen an Asian man that I cared to give the time of day. Some women might feel the same, but probably none of them are Chinese like me.

Well, half-Chinese. My father's family is originally from Canton. My mother's family is Caucasian—a mix of English, Dutch, maybe even some Scottish. I'm what they call *hapa*, half Asian–half white. However, growing up fourth-generation American-born in a white, middle-class southern California suburb, I always felt that I was not just half, but all white. Just like my friends.

At a young age I formed assumptions and ideals about men. Men should be good-hearted, intelligent, hard-working, taller than me, musically talented and they should have a nice smile. Adventurous, a definite plus. I liked them white and I preferred them Jewish. Or so I thought, until I went to Hong Kong and *they* walked in. The Chinese journalists, that is.

I couldn't take my eyes off them. One at a time, sometimes two, they walked up to the front desk. But they didn't just walk in, they entered. They arrived at the desk with a purpose. I was transfixed by their smart designer black and gray suits. Every inch of them was polished from their no-nonsense haircuts to their expensive Italian shoes. Their briefcases were unscuffed and their cell phones kept professionally out of view. They, like almost all the men in Hong Kong, wore silver oval glasses. Maybe they needed the prescriptions and maybe they didn't. They looked intellectual. Distinguished. Complete. I didn't know their names, their dialects or their business. All I knew was that they were tall, dark, handsome . . . and Asian.

I just sat and stared as they signed their papers, every move crisp and confident. Unlike the other journalists in the room, they knew where to go and what to do. My gaze followed them down the hall to the left, where they disappeared into unmarked rooms, official government attendants close behind.

My brow tightened. Confusion overcame me and I hid in my guidebook. I didn't want to think about how I looked to them. My grandparents never taught me the Cantonese word for wet monsoon rat. I was wearing gray cotton leggings with a red poncho tied around my waist. My hair was a mess and covered with a baseball cap. My feet hurt and I didn't feel like being seen. My soggy umbrella fell off the couch and I pushed it under my backpack. I felt like Cathy, that pathetic comic-strip girl who never seems to have anything put together.

Then I heard American voices. My eyes lifted to three Caucasian guys sauntering down the hall. They wore jeans and khaki photographer's vests. Their tripods, gigantic camcorders and fuzzy microphones were slung over their shoulders. I knew their names were Jake, Mike and Jack. Had to be. Rugged names for rugged individuals. I wanted to go with them. I wanted to *be* them, roving Hong Kong for the perfect shot, the perfect story, fantasizing about a hostile Tiananmen-like outbreak that would bring home a Pulitzer. I imagined them pushing through crowds to get to Prince Charles or to get a shot of Governor Patten. A meeting with opposition leader Martin Lee wouldn't phase them because they did it last week and probably would do it tomorrow, too. Running and sweating and then drinking a cold beer with the boys at the end of the day.

The Chinese men came back and stood across from the Americans. A quake quivered and shook along my spine. I looked from one group to the other. Chinese composure. American ease. Chinese integrity. American enthusiasm. Why was I impressed now, when never before had I admired a tailored suit? A cell phone? A briefcase? An Asian? I put my guidebook back in my pack and sat up straight. The quake continued but my heart was still. I was separating, body and mind. I was opening up. Suddenly my blood was a river flowing through me. A thousand creeks ran in and around my body, encircling the island of my heart. The Chinese were proud. The Americans were comfortable. Now my body was flooding with emotion and I stood on my heart, the only solid ground.

I looked back and forth at them one more time, the Asians and the Caucasians. They didn't look at me. They didn't have to, they *were* me. I closed my eyes. When I opened them, they were gone. I had been lost in a mirror.

Alison came down the hall, without a pass but ready for the street. Hong Kong awaited. The next day the British were going to return their last colony to the Chinese. We had come for the handover, but now I knew . . . I had come to take back me.

The Place of Wild Tortoises

LYNN FERRIN

Why, please, subject myself to such an ordeal just to see some dusty old reptiles? Why rouse my moldy backpack from its comfortable hammock of cobwebs in the cellar, and adventure forth upon equatorial seas, trudge up the scorching sliding slopes of some wretched volcano and sleep in the dirt— just to gaze into those tired and noncommittal old eyes? Hmmmm?

Well, yes, the giant tortoises of the Galapagos Islands *are* unlovely—but still, some tiny atavistic corner of my soul compelled me toward them.

As children, we saw them in zoos; maybe, God forgive us, we rode upon their backs around a squalid pen. And something remained in the mind: Somewhere these creatures are born free, and live wild.

Or perhaps it is their poignant place in history. Without them, early sailors rolling on remote seas might have starved. They also had their role in intellectual history: Because they vary slightly from island to island, even volcano to volcano, they served as examples for Charles Darwin, as he developed his theories of natural selection. The Galapagos Islands were named for the saddle-shaped shells of the tortoises that live on the drier islands and must reach up higher for food, so that their shells curve upward above their necks. (Those that live on more lush islands have dome-shaped shells for pushing through thick vegetation.)

Unlovely they may be with their scaly legs and reptilian wrinkles, but personally, I'm nuts about them: that sad E.T. face, that Darth Vader hissing, that sweet manner—despite their abominable treatment by mankind.

Once the giant tortoises numbered in the hundreds of thousands and could be found throughout the beaches and uplands of the Galapagos Islands, 600 miles off the coast of Ecuador. Then passing explorers and sailors discovered that the reptiles can live for as long as a year without food or water, and that they were uncommonly easy to catch. One simply picked them up and carted them away, although at up to 600 pounds it sometimes took eight men to carry one of them. They were stacked upside down, alive, in the dark, damp holds of wooden ships to serve as fresh meat on long voyages.

Now only a few thousand giant tortoises survive in the wild, and the largest concentration of them is found on the summit of

Volcan Alcedo, on Isabela, largest of the Galapagos Islands. Visitors to these islands usually come away believing that the only tortoises one can see are those in captivity at the Darwin Research Station on Santa Cruz, which has an ambitious captive-breeding and release program.

But if you are willing to carry a heavy backpack for five miles—and up 3,700 feet—you, too, can go calling upon the wild giant tortoises.

After some research, I signed up with an adventure travel company offering a Galapagos cruise that included the arduous climb of Alcedo. We would spend ten days on a sailboat, traveling among the islands in the usual style of Galapagos eco-tourists, hiking short distances to see the flightless cormorants, the dance halls of the blue-footed boobies, the rookery of waved albatross. Then our ship would drop us off on Isabela, at the trailhead for Alcedo, and return for us three days later.

Those first ten days, as it turned out, were beyond my wildest imaginings. Our vessel was the *Encantada,* a comfortable seventy-foot ketch with a scarlet hull and soaring rust-colored sails. The chef, Benny, slaved in the tiny galley night and day over delicious Ecuadorian meals. Our biologist guides, the Ecuadorian Macarena Iturralde and the Guatemalan Patsy Topke, were both possessed of a rich love for the Galapagos flora and fauna.

We snorkeled in the cool, clear waters with sea lions and penguins, snoozed on the warm decks, bantered on the beaches. And every now and then our ship would pass near Isabela Island, and we'd squint through the pink haze at Volcan Alcedo, an old lava flow licking down its flanks like a great black tongue.

From the sea, it looked like a very difficult hike. Half the people in our urban group had never carried a backpack before. Our number included a British widower with his two teenage daughters, a Manhattan investment banker, a psychiatrist, a writer and a J.C. Penney electrician from the Midwest. We ranged in age from sixteen to fifty-five.

The night before the climb, we nervously packed and repacked our gear—clothes, tents, sleeping bags, cook stove, food. The heaviest item would be drinking water for three days, as there is none on the volcano. *Encantada* didn't carry scales, but we estimated each backpack at something over forty pounds.

It was 5 A.M. and still dark when we dropped into the skiff and sped for the shore at Shipton Cove. We sat there in silence, a little scared, barefoot for the wet landing.

On the beach, I dried my feet, laced up my boots and struggled into my backpack.

Aaaarrgggg! My knees buckled. My spine seemed to be compressing. It was by far the heaviest burden every borne by my scrawny shoulders.

Time for a self pep-talk: Do you want to see those tortoises or blob around on the boat by yourself for three days?

Okay. Go!

For the first four miles of the Alcedo climb, the incline was steady but gradual, through a low forest of leafless gray *palo santo* trees. The last mile was a steep struggle up the outer flanks of the caldera.

The trek took us more than five hours; for the first hour we walked by the light of the waning moon and through the mellow dawn. Then the orange orb of the sun slipped from the sea and struck our backs.

Sweating and morose, we began the brutal push to the summit. The trail was deeply rutted, waist-high in places. Our broiling boots kept slipping backwards in the volcanic sand; we grabbed at the bushes for handholds.

I was whining to myself: Next year, Club Med.

Then, only a few yards above, Patsy's face beamed through the scrub. "I'm at the top."

By 11 A.M. everyone had made it to the rim, and we had settled into our Campsite from Hell. The thin, dry trees gave almost no shade, and when we fell to the ground to rest we were immediately showered with chiggers, hundreds of which had sprung to life to celebrate our arrival. We were smeared with grime, but water was too precious for any washing. We quietly ate our soggy sandwiches and crawled into our tents.

No one moved until late in the afternoon, when we slowly started looking around. Our campsite was perched on the east rim of the crater, which appeared to be about four or five miles long. To the south, the windward rim was luxuriant and green, moistened by the *garua,* the mist that hangs over these islands from May through December.

It is in this area, where there is plenty to eat, that wild giant tortoises can be found in the greatest numbers. Below the green rim rose a white column of steam—an active fumarole. Near where I stood, a vermilion flycatcher was performing territorial diving from the rim, trying to impress some hidden lady love. If she was not enchanted with this daring little packet of fire, I certainly was. I stepped over to the outer rim, with its panorama of other islands, other volcanoes. The sea had a dull shine, like a great pewter plate. And there, miles below, I could make out the *Encantada,* still at anchor in the cove.

On one short foray before dinner, we found our first tortoises. They were medium-sized, snacking happily on some dry leaves, giving us nary a glance until we came very close. They retracted their heads, exhaling with a loud hissing noise. Other than the mating growl of the male, this is the only sound they make. We watched quietly, and slowly they emerged and continued to dine. They were close to camp. I recalled a friend whose Nikon had been flattened by a steamrolling tortoise, and made a note to hang everything important in the trees.

That night, after a meager meal, we stood on the rim looking out across a quilt of clouds, bewitched by the glorious sunset and then by the Southern Cross hanging low in the sky. We were in our tents and comatose before full dark.

Next morning we started walking south. Ahead of us, the *garua* mist spilled over into the caldera, looking very much like the fog-falls over Skyline Ridge, south of San Francisco.

We scrambled through a chasm known as Devil's Ditch, then followed a faint trail along the ridge. As we approached the *garua,* the landscape grew more verdant.

Before long we found a tortoise, chomping on a bush. We stopped to watch a moment. Then we saw another—a big one. The investment banker decided to keep count. The trees were taller, in full leaf, strung with dripping moss. The bare dirt was replaced with tortoise-trimmed grass, green as an English lawn. We saw three more tortoises, then ten more.

Obviously they had little fear of man. We had no idea how long it had been since they had seen other humans, but after their first surprise encounter with us, with the usual retractions and wheezing, they returned to their business.

Most of them seemed to be eating breakfast. A few were strolling along well-worn tortoise trails or lying in wallows, their feet splayed out. One stood high on its legs, neck stretched full out, while a finch tidied up by removing its ticks and other parasites.

A braying sound shredded the silence. Ahead of us, four wild donkeys galloped up the ridge, paused to watch us, then disappeared.

We were not happy to see them. They are one of the many feral animals introduced by man which threaten the survival of the tortoises. Donkeys trample the tortoise nests, crushing their eggs, and compete with them for food. Wild pigs, dogs, goats and rats also take their toll in one way or another.

By mid-morning we had counted more than 200 tortoises, and all these were close to the trail and easy to spot. Who knows how many more we would have found with a little bush-whacking?

Then we decided to climb down to look at the steam fumarole—a drop of several hundred feet, so steep that we accomplished it mostly by sliding on our rumps, our arms and legs clawed by the brush. The fumarole was roaring like an irritated dragon with foul sulfurous breath.

The sun was hammering on our shoulders, and I dreaded going back up that slope. Instead we did something even more foolhardy, considering how little water we carried.

Patsy and Macarena mentioned that it might be possible to walk all the way around the caldera rim, although they had never done it. It would take us the rest of the day.

We decided to go for it.

We dropped from the fumarole to the crater floor, where a few donkeys trotted through the dead-looking forest.

We found several tortoises, but they were motionless, drawn into their carapaces, huddled together in the spare latticed shade beneath the trees. They had all the time in the world to do whatever they wanted. Undisturbed, they can live 150 years.

The cool green mansions of the *garua* were far above. I wondered if these tortoises had ever been there, or even knew it existed.

On the west side of the caldera we came across a field of sulfur vents with brilliant yellow crystals shining through the steam. From there we clambered up to the rim and continued our circle, sometimes following donkey trails, sometimes just instinct. All the way around the caldera rim we found tortoises—or evidence of them. The investment banker was too tired to count after 258.

By late afternoon we were out of water, crabbing at each other in stupid arguments, our feet screaming. Two people got lost, then found the route again. It was twilight when we stumbled back into our miserable camp, one by one. We had covered more than a dozen miles, blasted by the sun, and we were unbelievably filthy. I had a blister that had taken on the dimensions of another toe. The guides said that, as far as they knew, no other tour group had ever walked around the rim of Volcan Alcedo.

There was another night of exhaustion, insects, a horrid dinner in that enormous silence between the clouds and the stars. In the morning we packed up, and limped back down to the shore and bathed in the tranquil bay while sea lions played around us like friendly dogs. Then we were feasting aboard *Encantada* and sailing away on freshening seas.

Now I'm back in my world, where the refrigerator is full and the water flows from gleaming chrome. My backpack reposes in the cellar, and the spiders are spinning.

I think sometimes of the gentle tortoises lumbering around the rim of Volcan Alcedo in the heat and the pouring mist and the flooding moonlight. It is a hostile place for mankind, and we have no business there, except for short visits to see the wondrous animals.

It is the place where the giant tortoises live.

I wish them well.

Spirits of Scotland

CATHLEEN MILLER

That first night on Skye, I slept peacefully in a lovely room decorated with 104-year-old cockatiel-covered wallpaper, fine British antiques and a comfy wing-back chair, which I pushed against the door. On top of the chair I piled four suitcases, artfully arranging them at a precarious angle so that the slightest jar would topple them onto the floor. Kerby—my husband of days—tried to push the carved walnut dresser in front of the door as well. But when it groaned in objection, he decided it would be a shame to damage a piece of furniture that had resided in Scotland since the time of his ancestors.

Kerby and I had decided to honeymoon in Scotland to celebrate our shared Celtic heritage. But the waning end of the trip had found us heading west in a hurry, stopping on the Isle of Skye only because the next step would plunge us into the Atlantic. Emerging from the tangled green vines and pink rhododendrons of the Highlands, we boarded a ferry under the ancient sentinel of Eileen Donan castle and crossed the flinty water to Skye. There we drove into town, carefully navigating the erratic path between newborn lambs and sea-beaten boulders heavy with the knowledge of the ages.

In Portree, we came upon a two-hundred-year-old stone manor house that, like many in the region, had been converted into an inn. Kerby opened the massive door, and we walked through a menagerie of stuffed badgers, bobcats, lynxes, foxes and Bengal tigers lining the dark hallway. Stopping next to an enormous, ornate East Indian gong, we rang the tiny bell at the reception desk. A balding red-haired gentleman dressed in a tartan kilt and a starched white oxford shirt answered. Obviously the descendent of one of the portraits (which I checked scrupulously for moving eyes), Mr. Hugh MacDonald showed us upstairs to his last available room.

That evening we dined downstairs with the other guests, sitting around the massive table like gentry of the manor. After hours of manhandling the MacDonald family silver, we introduced ourselves to a young couple visiting from Edinburgh, and we asked them to suggest a place to stay on our upcoming visit to their city. Beaming proudly, they announced that they knew the exact—the ultimate—indeed the perfect place for us. This lodging was a singular apartment above a restaurant known as The Witchery. It seems the flat was renowned as the former secret meeting place of a witches' coven; today it's available to a select clientele of intrepid travellers. My husband turned pale, and I wondered for the hundredth time on this trip what was happening. Thanking them for their advice, we went upstairs to bed and secured the door.

Ever since arriving in Scotland I'd had a strange feeling that I'd worked hard to ignore: This rugged country was not just alien in the way of a foreign land, but rather it was supernatural. I was irritated by this notion—as if I'd read one too many travel brochures trying to pique interest with hysterical copy: *Experience the dark mysteries of Scotland! Drink with the Druids! Sleep with the witches!* My intellect and emotions played tug-of-war and, each time logic edged me back toward center, a new Scottish encounter would drag me over the line and deep into the dirt . . . but this is British Style.

This was my first visit to the region, and I expected to find a more sparsely populated version of England. Instead, I felt I'd fallen into some pixilated land. If I turned suddenly I would see wood nymphs peering at me from behind trees. If I sat quietly in the woods ghostly figures in hooded robes would silently gather in a circle. The elusive, unshakable sensation of being in the midst of forces I could neither define nor explain persisted throughout my trip and still haunts my recollection.

God knows Scotland's spiritual history provides much nourishment for the imagination, and as Kerby and I traveled throughout the country this history came to life for us. In the unspoiled wilderness I could understand the inspiration for the beliefs of the ancient Druids. They derived their powers from nature—watching the solar system for indications of the future, merging their bodies into the trunks of trees, transforming themselves into serpents and birds. After days of being separated from urban life these concepts did not seem so bizarre.

Today, however, the majority of Scots are Presbyterian—or so they say. I couldn't shake the feeling that in secret they were still pagans, sneaking off to the woods to worship the sun and inhabit the trees. The natives seemed like an otherworldly, mystical people possessing a patient, superior knowledge far beyond the mundane wisdom of Presbyterianism.

During our visit I was reminded often of Scotland's long obsession with witchcraft. Once we stopped at a quiet tea room on a deserted country road and found a large number of books on witchcraft for sale. Shocked, I scrutinized the waitresses for any tell-tale signs of witchiness. After leaving Skye, we explored the cobblestone streets of Old Town Edinburgh until we came upon a fountain on Castlehill that marks a favorite execution spot—a morbid reminder of the thousands of men and women who were burned at the stake or hanged in the fifteenth and sixteenth centuries as witches. The victims ranged from poor village women who used herbs to cure the sick (thereby threatening the sovereign healing powers of Catholic priests) to wealthy landowners possessing irresistible real estate. It just so happened that the state inherited all land upon a witch's execution.

Staring at the spot where so many victims met their end, a vivid nightmare I'd had as a teenager flooded back. The setting of my dream was the Middle Ages, on a day of wintry morning sun. I was being drawn in an ox cart down a rutted dirt road. My hands were tied together, and as the wagon lurched I was unable to keep my balance. My rough woolen garment chafed as I bounced along. The peasants lining the road screamed taunts and hurled rocks as I passed. Then the executioners jerked me from the cart, led me to the top of a small hill and bound me to a post. As they piled straw around my feet I struggled vainly against the stiff ropes, trying to get free. Efficient, businesslike, purposeful men—they set the straw on fire. The gas and smoke rose in a circle around me, blurring the horrible screaming mouths and contorted faces and distorting them into elongated, liquid flickering ghosts that sizzled and evaporated into wavy tracers of evil, rising toward the heavens. The heat closed in on me; my heart pounded Brit style. Feeling betrayed and desperate, the words "please don't let it end like this" throbbed in my head. The searing blaze bit into my legs and as the pain shot upward, a scream started in my flaming feet and traveled with the fire up my limbs, spreading like molten mercury through my veins, until I wailed like a banshee. I woke from my nightmare screaming, to find my bedroom suffocatingly hot, the sheets on the bed soaked with sweat. Standing in Old Town Edinburgh, I had a great deal of sympathy for those who burned here on Castlehill.

But my experiences visiting Edinburgh and Skye might not have fazed me so much had it not been for our adventure in the Highlands, where things were undeniably strange.

As we drove west from Inverness, Kerby spotted an old, gabled stone hunting lodge with a small bed-and-breakfast sign. Separating the lodge from the road was a velvety green pasture where horses grazed. He jerked the rental car into the driveway and said, optimistically, "This looks like a nice place, huh?"

"Hmmm, yeah. *You* see if they have rooms. I'm staying in the car." I was disgusted because after I'd exhausted myself planning our wedding, I'd arrived in the U.K. to find my new husband had made almost no arrangements for our honeymoon. "Wait a minute, planning the honeymoon was YOUR job!" I'd cried.

"We'll wing it," he shrugged. On this particular day, "winging it" had meant that instead of having any fun, we'd spent several hours driving through the Highlands stopping at all these great B&Bs—only to learn they were all full because it was Bank Holiday weekend. Grouchy and sullen, I stared out the car window planning how I'd let my husband sleep in the front seat with the gear shift up his butt. But he returned smiling and announced he'd gotten us a cozy room up in the garret.

"You'll love this place!" he promised as he grabbed the luggage from the trunk. Kerby, who is normally a whiz at directions, could barely find his way back to the room through the maze of hallways—upstairs, downstairs, winding through narrow corridors and then back upstairs again. I was charmed by the quirky old place but vowed never to venture out by myself, since I have problems finding my way out of a restroom stall. I knew if I left the room alone they'd find me days later, huddled in a linen closet somewhere, miraculously surviving on a diet of tea towels and wallpaper scraps.

Now that we finally had a place to spend the night, Kerby offered to buy me a drink to make amends. We ventured into the nearest village, Fort Augustus, where we discovered a few shops clustered around Loch Ness, and walked across a small drawbridge to a local pub called the Lock Inn. We knew we'd found the hot spot of town even before we entered. On this weekday afternoon, whooping war cries emanated from within, and wobbly patrons tumbled out as we opened the door. The room was warm with wood and the old-fashioned trappings of a public house that has seen many a toast up and down the long bar— which today held up several happy Scots.

We began sampling a few pints of the local ales and met some of our fellow drinkers. The bartender was a young man from New Zealand, who seemed to find the whole scene as amusing as we did. Soon Kerby and I learned that one of the great things about drinking in that establishment was the complete lack of pressure to remember anyone's name. I was the only woman in the place, and all the men were named Donald. As afternoon turned into evening, we accepted the tutelage of our new friends and began to sample some of the finer, unusual Scotches available. Normally I consider drinking Scotch a treat akin to drinking hemlock, but I reasoned when in Scotland . . . The sounds in the room began to ebb and flow like the waters of Loch Ness lapping at the draw-bridge. They rose to a sharp crescendo, then receded into soft slurring, cooing, contented murmurs that flooded through cracks in the paned windows to swirl around the pylons of the bridge. My cheeks burned with the fever.

Suddenly I became alert, my senses surging with "the feeling" again. I whirled around from my fixed position at the bar to look dead into the electrifying blue eyes of a very short man, barely five feet tall. He had spiky brown hair and a look of keen perception on his angular Scottish face. I was so shocked to find this strange person standing inches from me, staring at me intently, that I gasped involuntarily. He introduced himself as Donald Donald. Well, no surprise there.

While my husband stood a few feet away talking with a hydro-electric engineer from Wales, Donald Donald and I launched into a lengthy, bizarre conversation in which he told me of his strict religious upbringing on the Isle of Harris. He'd been raised by his grandmother, a woman governed by an odd combination of reli-gion and superstition. Donald had spoken only Gaelic as a child, an admission supported by his thick accent, which was marred by the abrupt starts, stops and high-pitched grinding of a truck stuck in the mud. He described joining British Special Forces and learn-ing how to kill a man in ten seconds using his bare hands. After he'd killed his third man he left Special Forces, and now he ago-nized over his past sins and their conflict with his grandmother's teachings. Even though Special Forces tried to lure him back, he struggled with unemployment rather than despoil his soul any further. He thought about killing himself. And he drank a lot.

Oddly enough, he'd also been waiting to meet a woman like me all his life. I pointed out that his timing was bad, since I was on my honeymoon, and my husband was standing right behind him. I seized upon this opportunity to introduce him to Kerby. Donald Donald was a good sport, I'll say that for him, and he and my husband got along famously. At some point he informed us that his grandmother had taught him how to read palms, and he began to read Kerby's. It predicted a long life, prosperity and a second marriage. Then he looked at my right hand. Nothing too spectacular there.

When he looked at my left hand we watched his face turn white, as if he might faint. "What is it?" I demanded as he dropped my hand like a jinxed talisman. He shook his head violently and refused to talk. Amazed, Kerby and I both insisted he explain. Finally Donald demanded, "Do ye know about this hand?"

"It's my left hand—I know it doesn't work very well. What are you talking about?" I asked in alarm.

"Six six six," he hissed.

"Six six six?"

"The sign of the devil!" he spat out, beginning to back away, his hand raised to shield against the spread of evil. I looked at him, then at Kerby. It was evident that the still-shaking Donald was not joking. His wary eyes riveted on me, lest I try to shape-shift into a cat—or a brew.

"What are you talking about?" I pleaded, trying desperately to find something humorous in this and failing completely.

"Lass, ye have the sign of the devil on yer hand. I don't know what ta tell ye. Do ye go to church?"

"No."

"Well, ye better start! And ye better pray. Cut your nails and pray!"

In spite of this unsettling declaration, we continued to talk and drink Scotch until Donald Donald lurched into a spasm and collapsed, ramming his head into the bar in the process. Several of the regulars rushed to help him to his feet. Then, as the bar was closing, he invited everyone back to his place, including Kerby and 666.

We followed Donald in our car to a location on the outskirts of town and parked in front of a tiny rusted trailer. The electricity was turned on by a coin-operated meter, and I waited inside alone while my husband and Donald put change in the box. Kerby watched Donald leaping at the meter—which was far above his head. Finally my husband put the money in, and when the lights came on, he saw the ground below the box was already covered with coins that hadn't quite reached their mark.

Inside, the dim bulb reflected a soft, greasy glow off the wood-grained vinyl paneling. The light revealed a rough-and-tumble bachelor's digs—a shelter devoid of any but the most utilitarian elements: a tan plaid sofa, a television, a toilet that had seen years of abuse. Yet Donald was prepared for guests, with cases of warm beer conveniently stacked in the living room. As we awaited the arrival of the other guests he told us, "I knew ye were comin' due ta a dream I had last night. Two white snakes crawled out of me carpet and when I saw ye tonight I knew it was you." While imagining myself as a white snake, I caught our host looking at me longingly. Donald Donald was soon joined by several other Donalds and a woman we learned was the chambermaid at our inn.

Someone turned on the television and Kerby and I laughed when we saw what was playing: Elvis Presley's 1968 comeback appearance in Las Vegas. As the King sang, everyone began to dance. I marveled at the absurdity of the moment, that I should be in this tiny trailer in the wilderness of Scotland, dancing with my husband and a roomful of assorted Donalds to Elvis Presley on television.

Black. Cold. Bare feet on a stone floor. I was walking in total darkness. I reached out my hand to find my way and touched a rough rock wall. Where was I? I realized I was having a nightmare and rolled over to go back to sleep. Except I couldn't go to sleep because I was standing up. And I was walking. And I was very, very cold.

I felt my way down the crypt-like corridor blindly, unthinkingly. I didn't know where I was going, but only knew that I had to go. I was a puppet, pulled steadily along by a piano wire of steel. Slowly I began to wonder where I was. What was happening? Where was Kerby? Where was Donald Donald? Why was I in this dark place alone, I who am terrified of the dark? Why was it so cold? It was then that I realized I was completely naked.

Growing alarmed, I tried to imagine what had happened. Was I dreaming? Why did Kerby leave me in this strange place by myself? Something must have happened to him. Maybe Donald had killed him with his bare hands so he could have me all to himself and had imprisoned me in some secret crypt only he knew about. Maybe he decided to do the world a favor and get rid of the demon 666 by locking her in a dungeon. Maybe he had killed Kerby, was going to kill me, then himself. These thoughts played silently through a far-away corner of my mind, as a guiding force continued to propel me onward.

My outstretched hand touched a door. I opened it and found stairs with a dim light coming from above. When I reached the top of the stairs I saw a red tartan carpet—the carpet at our inn. I walked across the deserted lobby and strolled into the sitting room. I didn't have to wonder how to find my way through the maze back to my room. The force was guiding me. The spirits of the house laughed as I floated helplessly in their grasp, up the stairs, around the corners, until I stood in front of the open door to my room. I closed it and lay down next to my sleeping husband.

In the morning I told him of my nocturnal adventures. At first we tried to laugh it off as only a crazy dream, but as the day wore on and I supplied more and more details, we both realized it was not a dream. I accurately described portions of the inn Kerby had visited alone when he booked the room. Never admitting we were frightened, we joked and proceeded to pack. Then we jumped in the car and fled as far from Fort Augustus as the geography would allow. We drove to the end of the continent, boarded the ferry, then drove some more until we reached the outer Hebrides. During our hours in the car, I felt sorry for my new husband. It must have come as a rude shock to learn he'd just married Devil Woman. But he took it in stride and I decided this somewhat evened the score for his inability to plan a honeymoon. I vowed to be nicer to him.

For months after we returned home, I tried to make sense of what happened in Scotland. My experiences there might have been odd glimpses of a past life, the product of an overactive imagination or simply the rewards of too much Scotch. But finally I decided to simply savor my memories of the trip as souvenirs of a wild and unpredictable place. I remind myself that Kerby and I went to Scotland to discover our heritage. God knows, we got more than we bargained for.

Taking Dedecek Home

DANIELLE MACHOTKA

The cemetery at Vysehrad, on the outskirts of downtown Prague, is where Dvorák, Mucha and most of Czechoslovakia's other prominent artists and writers are buried. Originally the site of the Prague castle, it sits on a high rock overlooking the Vltava River. Human-sized polished granite headstones stand in neat, flower-filled rows, surrounded on three sides by a colonnade, and anchored on the fourth by a small church. As people navigate the narrow paths, their faces move in and out of the sunlight, mirroring the rhythm of the trees that preside over the silent congregation.

We arrived in the mid-afternoon of a clear, cool day in early May. The lilacs, which are ubiquitous in Prague, were in full bloom, lending a sweet perfume to the air. A few people quietly wandered among the rows of graves, paying their respects to loved ones, or perhaps to those whose poetry or music moved them. Singing unseen in the trees, a thrush accompanied the conversations of a small group that was gathering near the colonnaded walkway, chatting enthusiastically. We approached the assembly, and within fifteen minutes I was introduced to more Machotkas than I thought existed, a situation that was emphasized by the Czech custom of introducing oneself by last name.

"Machotka," the men said as they held out their hands.

"Machotková," said the women.

"Machotka."

"Machotková."

Machotkas and Machotkovás had come from all corners of the Czech Republic for this occasion. Their warm smiles confirmed that we American Machotkas had been missed and were being welcomed home. We had known about each other, the Czech and American sides of the family, but most had never met. Events that had taken place fifty years earlier had dictated that there would be an American branch of the family, and now that branch was slowly being grafted back onto the tree from which it had broken.

Dedecek (the Czech word for grandfather) worked tirelessly for Czechoslovakia's freedom during World War II, collecting data for transmission to the government in exile and helping to organize the uprising against the German armies. However, the post-war Communist government viewed him as a threat to their fledgling rule, and concocted a trial in which he would certainly be jailed and possibly sentenced to death. He and Babicka (grandmother) left Czechoslovakia in 1948 with nothing but their children.

Separated during the escape, the family met again in Germany and came to the United States, where Dedecek died and was buried in 1970. He never again saw the country for whose freedom he had worked so hard. My father returned after the fall of Communism, and became acquainted with some of his father's surviving colleagues and students. It was they who asked my family to bring Dedecek's ashes home, to rest at Vyehrad.

Three trombones and a tuba solemnly marked the beginning of the ceremony. Dedecek's brass urn sat on a small table in the colonnade, on a black cloth decorated with red and white carnations and sashes in the tricolor of the Czech Republic—blue, red and white. An American flag covered the urn. Below it, a card read simply, "Dr. Otakar Machotka." Two men stood soberly on either side of the table; my father and one other gave the eulogies. Although the entire ceremony was in Czech, the sentiment transcended language. Dedecek had been a gentle, principled man, and the words that were spoken expressed both fondness for him and respect for his accomplishments. It felt less like a funeral than a graceful celebration of his life.

I looked around at my newly discovered family. People looked thoughtful but not unhappy; there were no tears. Instead, we listened attentively, even those of us who understood none of the words. Whether we spoke the language or not, we all understood the emotion in the eulogies and felt a collective sense of rightness in burying Dedecek here.

The ceremony was calm and dignified, culminating in the moment when my grandfather's life finally came full circle. My father carefully lifted the American flag from Dedecek's urn, while one of the Czech men draped the Czech flag over it, quietly, without comment. All of the feelings that had been surfacing slowly since I had arrived streamed down my cheeks as if they had been trapped for twenty-eight years. I looked around and realized I was not alone. Handkerchiefs and tissues appeared out of pockets and purses to dab eyes that had been dry until now.

One of Dedecek's compatriots picked up the urn, wrapped in the Czech flag. It was heavy, and the strain was obvious in his face, but the significance of the event gave him a strength that allowed him to carry it with touching dignity to the now-open grave, and set it gently on the edge. A few more words were spoken, and everyone broke into the Lord's Prayer, familiar even in a foreign language with its rhythms and intonations. I mouthed the words in English.

The man who had carried the urn to this point then laid it in the grave, next to the urns of five other people from Dedecek's small Social Democratic party. I said good-bye to him for the last time, yet I was moved more by joy than sorrow. This is exactly the way his story should end, I thought. Ninety-six years after he was born here, forty-seven years after he was forced to leave, and twenty-five years after he had died in an adopted country, he was at rest, at home among his people in the Czech Republic.

The Khan Men of Agra

PAMELA MICHAEL

One good thing about monsoons: They sure keep the dust down, I thought to myself, peering out the milky window of the Taj Express. I surveyed the approaching station from my uncertain perch between two lurching cars, ready to grab my bag and disembark purposefully. Despite the early hour, the platform slowly scrolling past me was packed with people.

Of the dozen or so bony hands struggling to wrench my suitcase from my grip as I stepped off the train at Agra, perhaps two were porters, four or five were rickshaw drivers, three or four were taxi drivers, and maybe a couple were thieves. The sudden rush of mostly barefoot men in states of (un)dress ranging from rags to britches brought me face to face with the difficulty of "reading" a person's demeanor or intentions in an unfamiliar culture. What to do?

I already knew from my few days in New Delhi that I would have to choose one of these men—not because I didn't want to carry my own bag, but because I would be hounded mercilessly until I paid someone to do it for me. It's a defensive necessity, and an effective hedge for women traveling alone who must rely on their own wits and the unreliable kindness of strangers—the taxi-wallah as protector and guide. In Delhi, though, the competitive tourist market is based more on ingenuity and charm than intimidation. Many of the drivers had developed very engaging come-ons, my favorite being the rickshaw driver who purred, "And which part of the world is suffering in your absence, Madam?"

My reluctance to hire anyone apparently was being inter preted as a bargaining ploy. Several men had begun to yell at each other and gesture toward me, ired by the low rates to which their competitors were sinking for the privilege of snagging a greenhorn tourist fresh off the train. Not wanting to see the end result of such a bidding war, I handed over my bag to the oldest, most decrepit-looking of the bunch, deciding I might be able to outrun (or overtake) him if I had to and also because he had an engaging (if toothless) smile.

Triumphant, he hoisted my bag on top of his turban and beckoned me to follow as he set out across the tracks. For the first few minutes the old man had to fend off a persistent few rival drivers who thought they could convince me to change my mind by casting aspersions on the character, safety record and vehicle of the man I had chosen, whose name he told me was Khan, Kallu Khan.

Halfway through the station, in a particularly crowded spot, Kallu handed my bag to another much younger (and, I theorized), more fleet-footed man. "Hey, wait a minute!" I protested. "My cousin Iki," Kallu assured me. "So, what's he doing with my bag?" I asked. "Helper," I was told. I went into red-alert and quickened my pace to keep up with Iki and my luggage.

As we reached the street it began to rain again, part of the deluge/blue sky monsoon cycle to which I had become accustomed. Over my objections, Iki put my bag in the trunk of their car, a battered Hindustan Ambassador that was unmarked except by mud, no reassuring "Agra Taxi Company" emblazoned on the door. "Thief might steal suitcase in back seat, Madam," Kallu explained. I acquiesced—the dry shelter of the "taxi" looked inviting and I was worn down by the ceaseless demands on my ability to communicate, decipher, make decisions, find, respond, protect, etc., that travel entails, even in a four-star situation, which the Agra train station was decidedly not.

Once underway, my relief at having escaped the crowd and rain was somewhat dampened by my realization that I was on a rather deserted road with two men who were probably making the same kind of un- and misinformed assumptions about me that I was making about them. I peered out the rain-streaked window to my right to get my bearings and to take in some of the sights I had come to India to see. I was also tentatively toying with escape options. All I could see was a blur of red, towering overhead and as far into the distance as I could make out. The Red Fort, of course. I had done my homework, so I knew the walls were seventy feet high, surrounded by a moat. On my left was a long stretch of sparse forest, separated from the roadway by a crumbling, low iron fence.

Suddenly, Iki pulled the car over on the left and stopped alongside a broken place in the fence. Kallu got out of the passenger side and opened my door saying, "Now I show you something no tourist ever see, Madam."

"That's all right, let's just get to the hotel. Tomorrow is better," I demurred.

"Please Madam," he insisted and, sensing my concern about my suitcase, he added, "Don't worry, Iki stay here with your bag."

I was already chastising myself for being so naive and trying to decide how much real danger I was in when I looked—really looked—into Kallu's eyes for the first time. They were kind; kind and bloodshot, but kind. In an instant I made the sort of decision that every traveler has to make from time to time: You decide to take a risk, trust a stranger, enter a cave, explore a trail, act on intuition and experience something new. It is this giving oneself over to a strange culture or environment that often reaps the most reward, that makes travel so worthwhile and exhilarating.

As if to affirm my decision, the rain stopped. "Okay, Mr. Khan, you show me," I said. We walked down a muddy path through a stand of stilted trees, leaving Iki behind, smoking a *bidi*. My courage faltered a couple of times when I caught a glimpse of a spectral, loin-clothed man through the leaves, but I said nothing and slogged on, hoping for the best.

It came quickly and totally unexpectedly—an enormous mauve river, its banks aflutter with river-washed tattered clothes hanging from poles and vines—the work in progress of *dhobi-wallahs,* the laundry men. Directly across the river, luminescent in a moisture-laden haze, was the Taj Mahal, seen from an angle that, to be sure, few tourists ever see, and shared with affection by a man who clearly derived great pride from its grandeur. The monument's splendor was all the more striking, its manifest extravagance even more flamboyant in contrast to the faded homespun garments flapping rhythmically in the humid monsoon breeze. We could only stand there and beam at each other on the shores of the mighty Yamuna, the Khan man and I. I like to think it was a sweet kind of victory for us both.

Amazon Mom

LISA ALPINE

My first experience as a Mom was in the Amazon back in 1974 when I was twenty-one. I got a village of Indians plastered and they abandoned their kids to my care.

I had unintentionally purchased this maternal role for the price of one dollar. All I thought I was buying for that corruptible buck was the use of a dugout canoe. I wanted to explore the banks of the Rio Napo, possibly to find a dolphin-inhabited lagoon, or glide silently close to a turtle in its muddy burrow, or even pass under a boa lethargically wound around an overhanging branch. Stuff like that.

The novel *Green Mansions* had awakened in me an incredible desire to travel the waterways of the Amazon basin. I took a year and a half off to penetrate its green veil. On a map, it looked like the Rio Napo would lead me to the Amazon. I began my journey on a rattletrap bus over the Ecuadorian Andes and into the *Oriente* rainforest, where the Napo snakes its way into the Amazon River to join it near Iquitos, in Peru.

Luckily, I was in no hurry and could hitch boat rides. There is an unspoken rule of hospitality among the people in the rainforest who live in huts on stilts along the riverbank. Travelers are welcome to sleep in their houses because the jungle floor is far too dangerous at night. Even the floor of the hut where I slept the first night was horrifyingly alive. When darkness fell, creatures began to torment me. Vampire bats, which I'd always thought were a myth, dive-bombed my head looking for places to attach themselves for their nightly fill of blood. After injecting an anesthetic into their unaware host, they are free to suck away. They prefer toes and noses; other travelers I met had alarming stories of waking up with puncture marks on the tips of their noses.

Then a creature I will never be able to identify ran back and forth over me. It seemed to have claws like a chicken and it made snuffly rodent sounds. I curled up under my rain poncho and sweated out that first night. At dawn I approached the residents and begged them to sell me one of their hammocks—anything to get off the ground!

With my new hammock and a sheet of plastic in which I could wrap myself up each night like a burrito—safe from critters, but steamy hot—I continued down the Rio Napo, first with the postmaster on his monthly mail run, then with a trader. Each progressive *panga* (dugout) got smaller and the motors fewer as I traveled deeper into the jungle. My forward pace came to a stand-still in Pantoja, on the Peruvian border.

I was stuck in Pantoja for two weeks. The villagers were reserved and suspicious, but allowed me to hang my hammock in an abandoned hut where, they informed me, the last occupant had recently died. He had fallen out of his boat in the middle of the river and "one of those big-mouth fish ate him." I made a mental note not to swim in the river.

Back to the buck . . . I offered the man in the hut next to mine money in exchange for the use of his canoe. When I waved an Ecuadorian bank note in front of him, he looked puzzled. Canoe rentals were a new concept and it looked like money was, too. They had no use for cash—there were no stores and the passing traders took animal hides and dried fish for payment. In the end, however, he finally took my money.

I now had an activity to pass the time. I'd already attempted to tag along with the village hunter, but keeping up with him in the web-like jungle was exhausting. He ran low to the ground with his blowgun at his side. The vine-tangled canopy made the forest oppressively hot, buggy and slippery. I knew I couldn't keep up with him, so I abandoned any romantic vision of watching him hunt down a jaguar or thirty-foot snake, and headed back to the village alone.

Paddling the tipsy, cracked canoe turned out to be another frustrating experience. The river's current was unexpectedly strong, the sun merciless. Perhaps the hammock, with its nylon cords that cut into my back, wasn't such a bad place to spend the afternoons. I abandoned the canoe and headed back to my hut where I parked myself with a book, twice-read and dog-eared, in the hammock.

Then the children appeared. Suddenly, I was popular. They were approaching instead of hiding from me as they normally did. By ones and twos, they'd climb or crawl up the splintery steps and peer at me with big, dark eyes. No smiles, just stares. The small ones gripped the hands of their older siblings. I swung back and forth, the hammock rope creaking, cutting a groove into the beams. The kids inched forward.

Soon this baker's dozen of kids, aged two to fourteen, were yanking the hammock to get it to swing higher. The little ones crawled into its banana-peel shape with me. Giggles, tickles, chasing—they took over my hut and didn't leave. It felt like a day care center run by the Cat in the Hat.

One melancholy-eyed girl picked up my hairbrush and stroked my blond hair. The other girls gathered around. Lubina, of the sad eyes, pulled my blouse forward and peered down the front. She shook her head in disbelief and pantomimed that I was "white all over!" They each took a peek and had the same incredulous reaction.

At dusk, the kids still filled my house. Dinner. What about dinner? I didn't want to eat my can of tuna fish, which I usually just scooped into my mouth on the end of a Swiss Army knife. There wasn't enough to go around, so it was oatmeal for everybody. They scurried over the banister and down the steps to get their bowls. Blue clouds of thirsty Morphos butterflies exploded upward from the puddle edges as the children stormed past.

I went to my neighbor's hut to get some water. The interior was pitch black. Snorting punctuated the darkness. Raucous laughter rose toward me from the floor as I tripped over something. I lit a match and illuminated a huddle of thigh-slapping villagers, all howling as they pointed at me. Apparently I was the funniest thing they had ever seen.

They were rip-roaring drunk, thanks to me. Mr. "Canoe Rental" had turned his tidy fee into enough cane alcohol to get every adult in the village drunk for several days. He'd paddled like a demon to the Peruvian military outpost (one shack, two soldiers) and brought back a huge jug of the local brew.

I didn't mind being laughed at—that was nothing new—but I felt guilty. I had corrupted this capital-free village with my measly buck. I was the snake in Rousseau's garden.

It became apparent why the kids had clustered around me. They needed me. Someone had to care for them while their parents lolled about, bathed in tears of mirth. No mean drunks here, just comedians.

The adults were on their drunken sabbatical for several days. I got used to living with a dozen kids. I felt responsible for them and they were very affectionate with me. I developed mothering skills I didn't know I had. I told them children's stories in a language they didn't speak. I cuddled the little ones and made a bed for them in my hammock. I cooked odd stews of dried fish and

smoked monkey meat. We washed our clothes in the river together from log rafts. They showed me where it was safe to swim.
We splashed and dived and painted our bodies with green-gray
clay from the riverbanks. My dreams of heading toward Brazil and
Carneval had drifted away. I forgot my downstream quest.

By this time the adults had exhausted their alcohol. They were
sober and back on track, but the kids still stayed overnight and
hung out with me during the day. Lubina walked about in my
over-sized clothes and looked like Minnie Mouse strutting around
with a pair of my high heels on her tiny feet. I had become so
fond of her, and I had fantasies of bringing her home with me.

Then a military seaplane landed in front of our village.
Suddenly there was transportation available, and I had to decide
quickly if I wanted to accept an offer of a ride to Iquitos. The
pilot was shocked to find an American woman in such a remote
outpost and felt obligated to airlift me to Iquitos.

I hurriedly packed and, in the hubbub of an abrupt departure,
I didn't feel the tearing sense of leaving the children behind until
the plane was circling over the village and I knew I would never
be there again.

The jungle is amazing from overhead. River tributaries twist
like Shiva's arms through the green tangle. So much water, so
much growth. So far away. I hear that the Rio Napo has been
destroyed by oil spills over the last decade. Lubina and the children of Pantoja are adults now. I wonder where they live if they
can live there no longer.

Lawrence, Cortes, and the Attraction of Gold

LINDA WATANABE MCFERRIN

Cuernavaca is a city of stone. The silent courtyards and well-tended gardens of its grand residences are encircled by thick walls of granite that separate the lives of their inhabitants from the filth and noise of the streets. Like most great colonial cities, it is a city of wealth and squalor. The affluent lounge in seclusion, while on the rude hills around them, shanty towns of corrugated tin crowd one another and mothers draped with infants squat by a river that carries raw sewage, drinking water that the cynical rich claim is "laced with protein."

We arrived in Cuernavaca by way of the Old King's Highway, in a station wagon that looked like it had been attacked by a can-opener. Traveling south from Mexico City, we crawled past fields of sugar cane and rice, through maguey-haunted landscapes. The car belonged to Arturo, our shaman-like guide. At the dusty turn-outs that passed for villages, gap-toothed *niños* swarmed us, thin arms reaching through the car's open windows, hands full of *chiclet* (gum) for sale. Arturo told us the children ate rice and corn flour and beans and then more rice; that they often slept hungry; that they'd lost the hope of clear-thinking to that protein-poor diet.

I remembered my last trip to Mexico and a journey into a similarly desolate countryside on a Sunday to pick out a new maid for our Mexican hosts. The girl was twelve. This was her destiny: She would cook and scour and clean for a family with children older than she in a big house in Mexico City. That was years ago. This time I was traveling with Arturo, our philosopher-guide; a thirty-year-old teacher by the name of Cecelia McGruen; and Lawrence, the man I was in love with.

We did not go to Cuernavaca at once, but circled around it, exploring the nearby attractions. Arturo was dealing a series of tales like cards from a soothsayer's deck. He conjured the Olmecs, the plumed god Quetzalcoatl, Spanish *hidalgos* and the ancient city of Tula. But I listened with only the slightest attention. My focus was fastened on Lawrence. Lawrence leaned on the frame of the open window, letting the wind cool his sunburnt eyelids. Under the narrow brim of his Panama hat, his eyelashes looked golden. His beard and mustache, ignited by the bright sunlight, made him look as though he were fashioned of gold, and I thought of Cortes as I studied Lawrence with an Indian fascination.

In 1517, when Hernan Cortes arrived on the Yucatan coast—his mission to conquer and lay claim to all he encountered for Spain and the True Cross—the Aztec leaders thought he was one of their gods. They thought he was Quetzalcoatl. They were waiting for Quetzalcoatl to return from the east. Cortes had golden hair and a beard and weapons and armor like they'd never seen. He had plumes on his shimmering helmet. He had an army behind him, and he drove toward them in magnificent sail-slung vessels over the eastern sea. He rode the horizon like the sun rides the eastern horizon at dawn. He was the personification of prophesy. They thought he was the Second Coming. They thought he was Quetzalcoatl.

But all that blond Spaniard wanted was gold. Maybe he wanted other things too—fame, glory—but they were all wrapped up in the gold. The Indians gave him what he wanted. They fulfilled his dream, as he fulfilled theirs. So two pieces of destiny met, as they were certainly meant to.

Cortes/Quetzalcoatl, the plumed serpent, destroyed the Aztec world. He brought death and smallpox and the True Cross. And the Indians filled his coffers with gold until the gold ran out. They gave him enough gold to stoke a fire under the desire for more gold. The desire could never be satisfied. They gave him a place in history and the death of his men.

"The name of this town we are going to see was 'Cuauhnahuac' in Nahuatl," our guide, Arturo, was saying. "It means 'place of the great trees' in the native Indian dialect. But the Spanish, they couldn't pronounce it. And they didn't know what it meant. They said the words sounded like 'cuerno de vaca.' So today this lovely city is called 'cuernavaca' or 'cow's horn.' Such a homely name for this beautiful spot. The place of the great trees is forgotten."

Cecelia waited a few heartbeats worth of time, then bombarded Arturo with questions. Her lank blond hair was plastered against her temples. She was cranky, too, suffering as I was, her legs covered by bites from the insects that teemed in the blackness of the bat caves near Lake Tequisquitengo, the Grutas de Cacahuamilpa. Whatever those bugs were, they were the same ones that lived on the flesh of the bats that slept in great hordes overhead. When we visited the caves Arturo had pointed a flashlight here and there, illuminating a fiendish architecture—fang-like columns of the still-dripping limestone that appeared to have been spun by a malicious troll. Cold drafts whined around them carrying, faint and urgent, a high-pitched squeaking.

"What is that noise?" Lawrence had demanded.

"Those, *señor*, are bats," Arturo had replied, flashing his beam briefly overhead, just enough to cause a crawling and teeming above us, and we saw that the cavern roof was furred with their legions. We did not, however, note the parasites that cohabited with them, nor did we feel them. But, when we left the caves, Cecelia and I, wearing skirts, looked down at legs covered with tiny red bites. These would grow to become open, itching mouths. Months later they would become scabs.

"Oh, these are attractive," I'd said.

"You could have warned us," Cecelia had scolded.

"*Señora,* how could I know that these invisible predators, so fond of bats, would find you to their taste, as well?"

Lawrence had looked at my legs with sympathy and offered the calamine lotion that was tucked into his luggage.

"No thanks," I'd replied. "They don't even itch."

I should have said "yet."

Cecelia asked if she could use some of the lotion and proceeded to slap it all over her legs. The car was filled with the mildly mentholated scent of zinc oxide.

"What did you say the Mixtec and Zapotec elements were in the motifs at Zochicalco?" Cecelia demanded of Arturo, bringing me back almost to the present. We had just come from Zochicalco, an archeological site significant because of the mixture of Mayan, Mixtec-Zapotec, Gulf Coast and Central Mexican themes. I'd been more interested in the bright red peyote buttons that tufted the hillside. Lawrence had pointed out the hallucinogen when he saw it.

"Look, peyote," he'd said.

"You mean the drug?" I asked.

"Yes."

On the heels of this revelation, two tour buses had arrived and disgorged their cargo of archeologists. Lawrence engaged some of them in conversation. They closed ranks around him, and he wandered with them through the ruins while Cecelia and I began our first tentative scratching, picking at bites.

On the road again, Arturo patiently explained the Mixtec and Zapotec influences to Cecelia, then turned to Lawrence and me in the back seat.

"Now we are going to Cuernavaca," he announced, "to pick up the fourth member of our party. But, since he will not be ready until three o'clock, we will have lunch, first, at a place that I know—the most exquisite place in all Mexico."

So when we arrived in Cuernavaca, we drove past wide avenues to a back alley street, Ricardo Linares 107, where ragged children sat in the road, playing around in the dirt. We knocked on a door. It was opened by a large man dressed in white. He looked us over suspiciously. Arturo mentioned a name. The man nodded. We were escorted inside. We were registered, there, in the dark vestibule, and another man, all in white, arrived and escorted us past the veranda and into a spectacular garden. Arturo did not come with us.

"No, no *señores*," he said. "I must wait here. I will go have my tortillas and come back for you when it is time to leave."

Lawn chairs and chaise longues were scattered here and there on the broad lawns. Knots of perfectly groomed guests chatted in groups of twos, threes and fours. Athletic young men in white moved between the groups with trays of drinks. Peacocks paraded around us. Monkeys hooted from ornate cages. Flamingos stood, practically like lawn ornaments, ignored by the wealth-weary guests. A dashing bronzed fellow came by and threw a spear with a red flag on the tip of it into the soft earth in front of us. A waiter asked for our drink order. Drinks arrived. Then, another white-clad waiter, who looked like an athletic trainer, rolled a standing blackboard up in front of us and recited the menu of the day. We selected our lunches. We were hungry, so we ate masses of food and got high on a Chardonnay that Lawrence selected.

We were still eating when Arturo returned to collect us and take us to the Cuernavaca Racquet Club where Will Decker, the last member of our party, was staying. Will was not ready. He was seated at tea.

"Please, please, sit down." Lifting a delicate china cup to his lips, Will addressed us. His deeply tanned wrist was dressed in a chunky gold watch. The hair on his arms glistened gold as well. If I wasn't already in love with Lawrence, I'm sure I would have fallen in love with Will. And it was a good thing I didn't. Love was nowhere on Will Decker's agenda.

Arturo grew more and more irritable. He wanted to reach Taxco before nightfall.

Once on the road again, we traveled for a long time in silence, climbing. The humidity thickened. Above us clouds loaded with rain gathered, muscled up to one another, rumbled threats, flashed lightning. The landscape darkened. The car coughed and wheezed as we climbed. None of us spoke. The grumbling skies and the station wagon's engine were the only sounds in the silence.

"*Señores* and *señoras,*" Arturo's voice slowly reeled itself out like a fishing line, baited and hooked, "have you ever wanted to kill anyone?" It was not an innocent question. His voice, a lazy sing-song, belied the intensity of the inquiry. He was like a cat purring, waiting to pounce.

"Arturo," I said, "that's a provocative question. But, I believe my answer would have to be 'yes.'"

"Only myself," Cecelia responded.

"I don't even own a gun," Lawrence confessed.

Will said not a word. He looked cramped in the back seat with Lawrence and me, not too pleased to be squeezed into Arturo's tin can of a car. Arturo looked up, turning his rear-view mirror so that he could see Will's reflection. We were all watching Will. And Will was watching the countryside, scanning parched plantings starving for rain. Then, his eyes swept the car, and he said with careless arrogance, "Kill someone? I've thought it. I've done it." And he turned stubbornly back to the thirsty landscape. I saw Arturo's eyes gleaming in the mirror.

"He's caught more than he expected," I thought.

I wanted to ask Will a million more questions, but his posture indicated that it wasn't a good idea. Cecelia looked frightened. I imagined, by now, you could crack a walnut between her petrified thighs.

So we sat as one often does, in life, with our unanswered questions on our lips and our expectations like unopened packages on our laps. We wound our way up toward Taxco in silence.

Cortes went to Taxco looking for gold. He'd heard that the Tlahuica, the Indians who inhabit the area, paid their debts in blocks of solid gold. In the eighteenth century Taxco became a boom town. Silvery, argonaut fortunes were built there. Remote, it stayed beautiful.

I'd been to Taxco before. One Easter, years ago, eight high school girlfriends and I had descended upon the town, unchaperoned. Still high from the bullfights, we were drunk with the exotic blossoms of Xochicalco; exhilarated by the ancient city of Teotihuacan, the "place of the gods," where we scaled the pyramids of the Sun and Moon; woozy with the Mexican romance novels that we used to practice our language skills; loaded down with baubles—Mexican shawls, hats and hand-tooled wallets; and hung-over from slamming back drinks in a country that would serve anyone who could belly up to the bar with the price of a shot.

The nine of us stayed at the Hotel Los Arcos, in rooms that were once monks' cells, and listened at night to the rattling chains and incantations of the candlelit Easter processions. The night was full of prayers to saints and virgins. It was full of chaste desires. Not surprisingly, of course, some of us were still virgins at the time.

No longer a virgin, I sat between two men in the back of a station wagon on this ascent to Taxco.

Will's moody power filled one side of the car, Lawrence's golden brilliance the other. As we climbed, I felt that we wobbled back and forth between the opposing axles like a misloaded carriage that was, at any moment, in danger of toppling over the road's edge and into the canyon below. A light rain began to come down, compliments of Tlaloc, god of rainfall. Taxco was as I remembered it—steep, cobblestone streets, the twin-towered coronet of the Santa Prisca Church, the pious accommodations of converted monasteries. When we arrived at our home for the evening, Cecelia peeled herself from her seat, headed straight for the lobby and then to her room, trailing a calamine slipstream. She promised to join us before dinner, at eight o'clock, in the lounge.

"You'll be eating at David's," Arturo advised us. "I know you will like it, *señores.*"

"Come on, Arturo," Lawrence pleaded. "You must join us for a pre-dinner drink."

"*Señores,*" Arturo demurred. "I am tired."

"I can't kick off the evening without you," Lawrence continued. "I need more of those spellbinding stories."

"Well, *señores,* since you insist," Arturo shrugged. He cast a smug look at Will, who was too busy with suitcase, camera and bags to notice. "I will join you."

"Great," Lawrence said. "Then we'll see everyone in an hour. We'll just put our bags up in the room."

Our room was white and monkishly simple. The floor was a rich red terra cotta. There were a few sticks of furniture made of charcoal-black wood and dry straw and a puritanical bed without bounce. But the room was large and full of warmth and the bed linens were a thick cotton, bleached blindingly white.

"Hardly the iniquitous den I had hoped for," I said sadly.

"It'll do," Lawrence replied, winding his arms around me. "These friars were a frolicsome lot."

We showered quickly, skin-to-skin, while outside the rain came down. We could hear it splattering off the veranda.

Lawrence lathered up—lean as a racehorse, high-strung and well-hung.

"Look," he said toweling me dry. "Let's play parlor games. Let's play pin-the-tail-on-the-donkey."

"All right," I said warily. "Where's the donkey?"

"You are, you nut," Lawrence laughed. "Come over here."

The monk's bed had only slightly more give than the terra cotta floor. There were no lights overhead. It had gotten dark. Just a table lamp and a couple of candles. We opted for candles and fell asleep side by side. I woke up to pitch black. Lawrence was awake, eyes wide, staring into the darkness.

"Did you see him?" he asked in a whisper.

"Who?" I asked.

"The Mexican Moses," he answered.

"Uh, oh," I thought, searching his face and sniffing the air for intoxicants.

I remembered the peyote on Xochicalco. Had Lawrence popped a few buttons or something?

"I saw a thin bearded man, in a huge sombrero," Lawrence said. "He was standing right there in the corner. The sombrero was electric. It had cacti with luminous spines all over it. Rattlesnakes wound their way over the brim. There were lariats on it, cattle skulls and bottles of tequila that glowed in the dark. He wore a serape. He looked straight at me. His eyes looked like water. I thought I'd fall into them."

This was very strange. Lawrence was conjuring visions like a starving mystic, and all I could think about was his downy ass!

"Lawrence, I didn't see any Moses," I said.

"Well," Lawrence replied, "I'd swear it was real."

"Just hallucinating," I concluded.

"Hallucination," Lawrence accepted.

"Lawrence," I reminded him, holding up my travel clock, so he could see the numbers and hands in the darkness. "What about Arturo? We can't stand him up."

"Damn, " Lawrence exclaimed, springing up. "Arturo. We'll hurry. Come on."

We dressed quickly and opened the door. The hot, floozy breeze gushed in. The night sky was curtained in lead and silver. Beneath it, the tile roofs of Taxco glistened, masked in watery shadow. We stood a few moments watching the sky prepare for the late-night pyrotechnics, then descended the steps and found our way to the cocktail lounge and Arturo. He had also changed clothes. He wore one of those Mexican shirts with embroidery down the front on either side of the buttoning placket. Cecelia was with him. She wore a Mexican blouse trimmed in lace. A colorful cotton skirt covered her bug-bitten legs. Will was nowhere to be seen.

"Anyone seen Will?" I asked casually.

"He is gone," said Arturo simply.

I thought I detected some pleasure in his voice. This was one more mystery to ponder.

Lawrence and I ordered drinks. Lawrence ordered a drink for Arturo. Once we had them, Arturo said, "*Señores,* you know I will not join you for dinner. I have my place and you have yours. But I'm glad you insisted upon a drink. It has been an interesting day."

"Yes," Lawrence agreed. "I just saw a Mexican Moses."

The fire leaped in the fireplace. Outside, raindrops exploded like small bombs on the swimming pool surface. Arturo did not even bat an eye at Lawrence's claim.

"You know, *señores,*" he continued calmly, settling back into his chair, "there are many witches in Mexico."

The Art of Darkness

CHRISTI PHILLIPS

The voodoo temple was lit by the warm glow of a dozen candles. Rivulets of smoky incense danced in the air. Loud, pounding rhythms of tribal drums pulsed through my body like a new heartbeat, one that reverberated in my chest, my hands, my head.

The voodoo priestess murmured incantations in French, her husky voice reminiscent of the black-haired siren in Jean Cocteau's *Orphée* who leads Jean Marais to the underworld.

"*A l'Esprit surtout,*" she crooned, "*royaume de Bon Dieu.*"

"*Ago, ago-é,*" the others responded.

The priestess held a small container of cornmeal as she kneeled before me, and asked if I would like to be anointed on my temples or on my neck. *Temples for inspiration,* she had told me earlier, *back of the neck for possession.* I indicated temples only, wondering just what I'd gotten myself into. I had come to the ceremony without expectations of otherworldly experience, but as the drumming and chanting continued I felt myself hypnotized by voodoo's entrancing music and ritual.

What happened next was something I never anticipated, and it convinced me of voodoo's inexplicable power.

My foray into the art of darkness had begun innocently enough. I was walking along Dumaine Street, feeling the French Quarter's aura of timelessness and decay that was accentuated by late summer's liquid, shimmering heat, when I saw the sign for the New Orleans Voodoo Museum.

I'd already peeked into some of the occult boutiques in the area. Along with an assortment of strange herbs, aromatic oils, and colored candles, the shops sold things such as "The Lucky Gambler's Best Friend" (muskrat jawbone, $3.95), a "Traveler's Protection Charm" (tiny bottle of Coca-Cola, $4.95), or a Ghana Ashnuti Tribe House Blessing Mask ($89.95). The Voodoo Museum, I'd heard, offered more than the usual collection of kitsch: It had something to tell, not just sell. I hesitated, unsure of whether I wanted to delve that deep.

I watched as three small boys, bottle caps pressed into the soles of their Nikes, tapped in syncopation then suddenly stopped and sat down on the curb, as if bored. Inside the empty cafe behind them, a ceiling fan turned slowly, barely stirring the torpid air. Two black-clad, much-pierced girls, pale and exotic as vampires, strolled arm in arm along the *banquette*. One story above, a woman in a tight blue dress stepped out onto her balcony and turned, eyes searching, to the river. The odor of stale beer and fried oysters mingled with the musky, damp smell of the Mississippi; the low bellow of a river barge underscored strains of music from a lone clarinet.

I felt New Orleans weave a spell around me, a spell I had yet to understand, as though the city held a secret beneath its surface. I felt it as a barely audible whisper, a phantom shadow at vision's periphery, a touch that tingled under the skin. Something in New Orleans lay beyond the five senses. Exactly what it was, I didn't know.

Perhaps voodoo held the answer.

Like most establishments in the French Quarter, or *Vieux Carré,* the Voodoo Museum is marked by a sign that hangs from a wrought iron rimmed balcony overhead. Unlike the others, an alligator head and broom handle above the narrow front doors keep evil spirits at bay. A painting of a regally beautiful quadroon woman, her head wrapped in a *tignon* and ears adorned with gold hoops, commands the lobby with a presence that rivals Mona Lisa's.

Alex, a young, earnest cultural anthropologist, led the museum's tour group. In a room containing a cemetery scene where candles burned to honor the dead, he began his spiel on voodoo by explaining what it was not.

"Voodoo isn't black magic, sorcery or devil worship," Alex said. "It's a religion based on spirit worship. The word *voodoo* itself is derived from the African Fon word *vodu,* which means 'spirit' or 'power'. Followers believe that there is only one god, but he's too remote to be concerned with the affairs of this world. Instead, they revere the *loa,* or spirits, who interact with people. Most voodoo ceremonies revolve around propitiating the *loa* and asking them to 'come down' to earth, in order to give help and advice. It isn't much different than praying to the Virgin Mary or to St. Peter; in fact, many voodoo practitioners are also Catholic.

"Over here," Alex turned to a display case, "is a collection of voodoo dolls, which work through a kind of spiritual acupuncture, by sticking pins in an effigy. Even though voodoo dolls are the most widely known aspect of voodoo, they aren't used much by real voodoo practitioners, who believe in karma. Putting hexes on people is dangerous business."

We passed through a narrow hallway that held a collection of paintings with voodoo themes. One depicted a voodoo queen biting the head off a chicken (animal sacrifice is often an intrinsic part of voodoo ritual).

"As you can see," he commented, "it's not always good to be the Queen . . . or the chicken."

The second room of the museum held two altars, one with a tattered top hat that belonged to Dr. John Creux, a voodoo priest of the 1800s. The second altar contained a bottle of white Puerto Rican rum, a crucifix, dried flowers, incense, a dish overflowing with pennies and plastic statues of Christian saints.

"The saints you see on the altar represent the *loa* and their Christian counterparts," Alex explained. "When African slaves were brought to the New World, they were forced into Christian worship. The slave owners didn't know that the deities the slaves worshipped were only stand-ins for the African gods. Over time, the saints and the *loa* became one; for instance, St. Peter is also Legba, the voodoo guardian of the crossroads; St. Barbara, because she wears a red dress and carries a sword, is also Shango, the god of thunder and war."

He pointed to a tall, hollow petrified tree trunk that stood next to the altar. "This is a wishing stump, similar to the one that belonged to Marie Laveau, New Orleans' greatest voodoo queen. You saw a painting of Marie at the entrance to the museum."

Born in New Orleans in 1794 to a white plantation owner and a Haitian slave, Marie Laveau was a free woman of color and a practicing Catholic who attended Mass every day in addition to presiding over voodoo rituals. Her many followers regarded her as their spiritual advisor and came to her to have a curse placed or removed or a prayer recited in front of St. Louis Cathedral. Marie was also a hairdresser who worked in prominent Creole homes, becoming a confidant to wealthy wives, husbands and mistresses. Not surprisingly, she was renowned for telling fortunes.

"The wishing stump was pretty straightforward. People wrote down a request, wrapped it around an offering—money, in most cases—and placed it inside the stump. Marie collected the requests and performed blessings."

He strode a feet few toward a glass cage. "This is Zombi, named after Marie's snake, Le Grand Zombi, who was an important part of her voodoo ceremony. When Le Grand Zombi licked her face, it was believed that she became possessed by Damballah, the *loa* of death and rebirth. At twelve feet long and 120 pounds, Zombi's too big to dance with, but he's an impressive mascot."

Alex led us outside to St. Anne Street, where Marie Laveau's house once stood. Along the way, he pointed out a few tall, cast iron poles with spikes at the top. Known as Romeo Catchers, the spiked poles were erected near the bedroom windows of Creole girls to dissuade suitors from secret nocturnal visits.

"Romeo on the way up, Juliet on the way down," he quipped.

Our next stop was St. Louis Cemetery No. 1, adjacent to the Iberville housing project. It stands atop what used to be Storyville, once the country's most infamous neighborhood. In the early part of this century, the Storyville Blue Book alphabetically listed over 700 "ladies of the night." Storyville was ironically named for Sidney Story, an alderman who tried to purge the city of its "sporting houses" by restricting them to a single area on the far side of the *Vieux Carré*.

Built in 1789, St. Louis Cemetery No. 1 is the oldest "City of the Dead" in New Orleans. Leading us on well-trod paths that wound through glowing white marble, pale granite and red brick tombs, Alex explained why all the burials were above ground.

"New Orleans is built on a swamp, and portions of the city are below sea level. Early settlers discovered that during heavy rains, bodies buried under ground float to the surface. As you can imagine, this was not pleasant."

The tombs were also efficient: The temperature inside rose up to 400 degrees, cremating the body. After a year and a day, someone else could be interred.

"The tombs aren't completely airtight. When bodies decompose, they release a lot of gas, and if the tombs were airtight, they would explode. For the most part, modern embalming techniques have taken care of this problem, but on a hot day, you can still smell something a bit odd in here. Hence the tradition of bringing flowers to a gravesite."

Soon we arrived at Marie Laveau's burial site, a tall granite tomb with a peaked top. Colorful, grafitti'd crosses and circles were chalked upon its surface. The crosses were drawn by seekers with requests; when their wishes had been granted, they returned to add the circles.

At the base of the tomb were offerings of Mardi Gras beads, flowers, coins and a Little Debbie Honey Bun that was swarming with ants. "Those beads have been here since Mardi Gras," Alex commented. "As you can see, people don't mess with the offerings. The weirdest stuff can turn up here . . . a while ago I saw a FedEx envelope." He caught my eye and grinned. "I wonder who signed for it."

The New Orleans Voodoo Spiritual Temple occupies a small storefront on North Rampart Street, not far from Louis Armstrong Park and what was, until the 1950s, called Congo Square. Slaves and free people of color were allowed to congregate in Congo

Square on Sundays to make music, sing, dance and perform rituals. During slavery, Congo Square kept African religion and music alive; after emancipation, the Sunday gatherings continued. The music played there incorporated African and West Indian rhthyms, minstrel melodies, slave work chants and the blues. Jazz, a syncretic form of music that adapted these musical styles and encouraged improvisation, was born in Congo Square.

Priestess Miriam, *mambo* of the Voodoo Spiritual Temple, offered me a chair in the middle of her *hounfort*, where followers gather for rituals. Surrounding us, numerous altars displayed offerings to the voodoo gods, and a glass cage held two large coiled, sleeping snakes.

A handsome black woman in her mid-forties, Priestess Miriam was first "touched by spirit" at the age of eleven, while worshipping in a Baptist church in Mississippi. After years of spiritual study, she was consecrated as Bishop at Angels Angel All-Nations Spiritual Church in Chicago. In her training she had studied the teachings of Moses, Jesus Christ and Mohammed, and revered them all.

"Spirit doesn't want us to be biased," she said. "There are many ways to Jerusalem. We all eat out of the same dish, breathe the same air, sleep under the same darkness."

Services offered by the Voodoo Spiritual Temple include palm, tarot card and African bone readings, as well as voodoo weddings and rituals, including a snake dance. Priestess Miriam's ceremonies draw a variety of people.

"Some come for the drumming, some for the setting. There are many wondering souls out there." She estimated that fifteen percent of the city's population regularly practiced voodoo. "Voodoo is a true religion that was demonized by Christianity. Spirit presents itself under voodoo, and it satisfies people. Some believe they need to prove that voodoo is a religion, but it doesn't have to be proven. If the spirit is there, it's true."

A large cardboard box near our feet suddenly rattled and hopped in the air. I jumped, wondering if this was a sign from the *loa*.

Priestess Miriam laughed gently. "Oh, that chicken," she said. "It startled me, too, earlier."

I ventured beyond the usual tourists' stomping grounds to reach the Island of Salvation Botanica, set in the midst of the shotgun houses, overgrown gardens and Po' Boy stands of the Lower Ninth Ward.

The botanica's owner, Sallie Ann Glassman, has been practicing voodoo since 1977. "The first time I saw some books about voodoo at a friend's house, I felt fear," she told me. "Then I realized that it was foolish to be fearful of something I knew little about. As I learned more, I discovered that voodoo is a healing religion. It offers a direct, immediate experience of the divine—something that's hard to find in our culture."

As a *mambo*, she had learned to go "to the doorway" that divides the spiritual and physical worlds, and call upon the *loa* for help on behalf of an individual or community. This drawing forth of the spiritual world into the physical was the primary purpose of voodoo ritual, one that sometimes culminated in possession— where a *loa* enters the mind and body of a practitioner. Most often, Sallie Ann was the one possessed, but it could happen to any one of the ritual attendees.

She invited me to her weekly voodoo ceremony, held in the altar in her house. I hesitated, thinking back to the doomed chicken in Priestess Miriam's *hounfort*. Sallie Ann assured me there would be no chicken decapitation, oral or otherwise. A strict vegetarian, she didn't believe in animal sacrifice. "I offer up *prana*, the life force, to the *loa* instead."

Sallie Ann answered the door wearing a long, white cotton dress and numerous strands of colorful *collares*, the bead necklaces of a voodoo priestess. The other members of her *hounfort* and I filed into a small, high-ceilinged room off the kitchen, and sat on the floor facing the altar. The candles had already been lit. As the door to the black-painted temple was shut, the effect was of a starless night lit by pale fire. A few attendees picked up congas and bongos and began to drum.

The ceremony began as Sallie Ann consecrated the room with water, and Shane, *houngan* of the *hounfort,* sliced the air with a machete. Then they engaged in a mock battle, he with the machete and she with her *asson,* a priestess's rattle with beads and bell attached. At the end of this ritual, a symbolic conquest of spirit over the physical world, they bowed to each other, and Sallie Ann kissed the hilt of the machete.

Each of us approached the altar one by one with our offerings for the *loa* in hand. As I'd been instructed by Sallie Ann, I made the sign of the crossroads in the air before placing my offerings—palm leaves and a small gourd—on the altar. I said a brief prayer for my grandparents and brother, my loved ones who had passed on, in keeping with voodoo's recognition of the spirit world.

Sallie Ann kneeled in the center of the *hounfort* to begin her invocations, calling on Legba, the *loa* that guards the crossroads between the physical and spiritual worlds. *"A Legba, qui garde la porte,"* she murmured, her voice blending with the rhythmic drums. She opened a glass container filled with cornmeal, taking a pinch between her thumb and fingers, and made the sign of the crossroads in the air. Slowly and precisely, she drew a *vévé*, a symbolic design that represents a *loa*, on the floor with cornmeal.

When the *vévé* was complete, it was oriented to the "the four quarters," south, west, east and north, with invocations and candles, water, incense and the *asson*. This aligned the ceremony to the elemental forces, and allowed spirit to descend.

A new drumming pattern began as Sallie Ann started another invocation in her low, sensual French. As she called upon the Marassa, or Sacred Twins, the Dead, and the Mysteries—"the invisibles who guide all things in the world"—I felt myself drawn in by the ritual, tugged by a timeless consciousness that responded as if from memory.

Sallie Ann took a mouthful of water and sprayed it over the *vévé*. The drumming intensified; the candles flickered a wan, yellow light and deep shadows on the walls. Kneeling before me, she rubbed cornmeal onto my temples; I felt the grains lightly brush my cheeks as they fell onto my shoulders. Then she shook the *asson* over me, beginning at my feet, then hands, then around my head. I heard the snake-like rattle of the *asson* in my ears, felt the throb of the drums throughout my body. It was an eerie sensation, and I was conscious of being changed in some fundamental way: a veil lifted, objectivity fell away.

The drumming and chanting grew louder; two people got up to dance, scattering the cornmeal *vévé* and welcoming the *loa*. The ceremony continued this way for some time, perhaps another hour. I saw it in a slightly hallucinatory haze, as if I were in a light trance. After I heard the *asson,* my memory of the voodoo ritual is imprecise; but I have not been able to forget what I saw, and heard, next.

While the dancers danced and the drummers drummed, I had a vision of a former love who had died years before, someone I hadn't thought of for a long time. He leaned against the far wall of the temple, and in a half-serious, half-joking voice asked, "Why did you not say a prayer for me?"

Later that evening I walked through the *Vieux Carré*. I'd had an experience I didn't quite understand; the last thing I'd expected from the ceremony was an encounter with a ghost from my past. But it was in keeping with the precepts of voodoo, which accepts and honors the dead as a living reality, as the *loa,* always present among us.

I looked up to see a flag bearing a skull and crossbones silently fluttering in the sultry night air. I felt my perception heightened, my senses sharpened, as if I were seeing the city for the first time. It was easy to imagine bands of iron-knuckled pirates roving through these streets, to imagine fine Creole ladies stepping out of ornate carriages, or languid, beautiful quadroon mistresses waiting in hidden courtyards for their lovers.

I felt the French Quarter come alive as it must have been 150 years ago, alive with the clatter of carriage wheels and horses' hooves, the rustle of taffeta skirts, laughter from honey-colored rooms lit by gold-plated candelabra, the clink of silver and china, slap of playing cards, rattle of dice, horn blasts and tinny music from river barges echoing through the streets. And beneath this, as primordial as Louisiana's bottomless swamps, were other sights and sounds: the throb of drumming along Lake Pontchartrain, the screech of a black cat, the silent slither of a water moccasin in a moonlit bayou. All were intrinsically bound together, as on a medieval wheel of life where birth and death effortlessly metamorphose from one to the other and back again.

I recalled what Andrei Codrescu had written about the city: "I had the fleeting thought that everyone returns to New Orleans; if they can't come back in their lifetimes, they come back when they are dead. I felt that everyone who ever lived here . . . are all still here."

Overhead, a neon sign sputtered to life, red letters flickering brightly against a background of cobalt-blue, swiftly darkening sky. The first word of the sign was burned out; only the second half remained.

"& Spirits," the sign proclaimed.

This was the secret that New Orleans held tight.

And spirits. And spirits.

Fast Luck

JENNIFER LEO

The dice flew from one end of the table to the other, rebounded off the end wall and teetered, everyone at the table watching until they steadied.

"Hard eight!" yelled the stick man. The table went into applause. Red, green and black chips stacked up as the house paid out.

I looked at the shooter. She was a cool, confident brunette in her late thirties, maybe early forties. She was no beginner but that didn't mean anything to me. It was all about energy. I tried to read her. What vibe was she giving off? I looked at the table and the number five called out to me. I looked up at the woman and confirmed the notion. She looked like five was her number. No reason, just a hunch. I put ten dollars on the "Come" line. Whether my intuition was right or wrong, it was bad luck to bet against a lady.

"Five!" yelled the stick man.

I knew it! I looked up at the shooter and tried to read her again. She was going to have a long roll. Long enough to make some money. I straightened my short skirt, twirled my earring and smacked my lipstick. Half an hour later I walked away ninety dollars up.

Except for knowing who's calling me before I answer the phone, my psychic abilities only show themselves when I'm gambling. Specifically, when I play craps. It started three years ago when my family had Thanksgiving in Vegas. Three generations made up of fourteen people shacked up at Bugsy Siegel's Flamingo Hilton for turkey day.

I didn't believe it when it first started. I was at the table hunkered down in my favorite corner spot next to the dealer. In my head whirled calculations of odds, box numbers and strategy rules to the system my grandfather taught me when I was twenty-one. As I stared hard at the numbers before me—four, five, six, eight, nine and ten—the six seemed to rise up off the table. It didn't fly or get up and run off the table. It just seemed to stand out from the other numbers. The next number rolled was a six. Coincidence? Then it happened again and again and again in different forms. Sometimes I just knew that a shooter would have a long or short roll. Sometimes I knew that the ten would come up. Sometimes I knew when the shooter would seven-out and end his turn. But I never trusted my intuitions and wouldn't bet on them.

This trip was going to be different. Knowing that my powers would be making an appearance with my first Vegas trip in two years, I planned ahead. Five days before my grand arrival in Sin City, I made a special visit to Curios and Candles, a San Francisco New Age shop that had been recommended to me. Denying any psychic ability and terminally fearful of becoming a crystal hippie if I did admit to any powers, I had always put this shop at the bottom of my to-do list. But now money was involved and I needed to win some. I wanted to enhance my abilities in any way possible.

As soon as I opened the door a sweet smell and calming music melted away all my apprehension. There were at least four other people in the shop keeping the clerks busy. I was as wide-eyed as any rookie would have been. In addition to the walls of books on astrology, spirituality, voodoo, myths and mysticism, there were candles, jewelry, charms, preserved snakes, crystals and—what I found to be most intriguing—jars of colored powder with labels suggesting they were potions. Some looked like love spells, others said "power," "black cat" or "peace." I fingered the mojo bags for power, confidence, love and luck. I needed all of them.

"If I can help you find something just let me know, Miss," said a man standing in front of the colored jars of witches' spells.

"Actually," I began, mustering all my confidence to talk about this crystal hippie stuff, "I'm looking for something to help strengthen my Power."

"Your personal power or higher power?" he asked.

"Uh . . . my personal power."

"What sign are you?" he asked next.

"Gemini," I said, as he sized me up.

"Well then, you need a purple candle. It'll be two ninety-five and forty cents for the blessing."

I doubted the strength of a blessing that cost forty cents. He returned with a purple candle the size and shape of the religious ones you can buy at the supermarket. Then he gave me a nail and asked me to scratch my full name, birthday and request to get in touch with my personal power on the top of the candle. Then he began the blessing by pouring oils from unmarked bottles on top of the inscription. After that, a sprinkling of silver glitter to attract the moon and gold glitter to attract the sun.

My eyes wandered to the potions. "What are those?" I asked, as he finished up with the blessing.

"Incense," he replied.

My eyes caught on a jar of bright yellow powder. In big black ink the label read "Fast Luck."

"I'll take some of that," I said, pointing to the big golden jar of hope and promise.

That was just what I needed for this trip.

"How fast *is* Fast Luck?" I asked. "If I need the luck on Friday, do I burn it Friday or Thursday, or when?"

"You should burn it every day this week, and especially Wednesday."

"Why Wednesday?"

"Wednesday is the day for money," he said.

How he knew I needed the luck for money I didn't know.

He packaged up an ounce in a small brown paper bag and rang it up for a dollar forty. This place was a bargain basement for all your wishes to come true! I thought for sure they'd be charging an arm and a leg, one way or another.

I went straight home and tried to light my new incense burner. The piece of coal wouldn't light. I went through a whole box of matches. Finally, I got out a second piece of coal and put it on top of the one that wouldn't work. It started right up. When it was starting to get hot, I added a little of the yellow Fast Luck powder to get the spell started. The burner flamed up a bit and then mellowed, giving off a sweet lemony scent.

Soon smoke rose out of the hole in the lid and out of the star-shaped holes in the side of the burner. Then it poured out of the holes. This was one powerful incense burner. After five minutes my roommate Oscar came in and said my room smelled like a barbecue.

"It's Fast Luck," I said, beaming, proud of my lucky charm hard at work.

All of a sudden the fire alarm went off. I went for the window as Oscar yanked the alarm out of the ceiling to turn it off. The burner was blazing hot and I used some old shorts to move it nearer to the window.

By now the room was filled with smoke and the incense burner was not letting up. It was starting to burn my wooden dresser.

"Oscar, do something!" I yelled.

"What am I going to do?" he asked.

"Throw it out the window." I was starting to panic.

He grabbed a towel and threw the flaming burner into the sink. My luck poured down the drain.

"Fire toys are off limits to you," Oscar said. "This is a sure sign of the luck you're not going to have on your trip." But I didn't believe him. Anyway, I still had the candle. I went into the family room and lit it up. It burned without a problem, turning my inscription into a purple pool of wax.

The next day I brought the Fast Luck to work and got my co-worker Susan to burn it for me. She was happy to do so since she'd be going to Las Vegas that weekend, too. More luck for everybody.

The craps tables at Caesar's felt like home. This was the first place I gambled when my grandparents took me to Vegas for my twenty-first birthday. I found a five dollar table and set up my bankroll of chips. I looked at the shooter. I read the shooter. I looked at the numbers on the board. The ten called out to me.

"Ten! Easy ten," called the stick man.

This time I was going to bet on my intuition. Sure enough, fast luck was with me that day at Caesar's. And at the Flamingo. And at the Stardust. And at the Stratosphere.

It's a Man's World

LYNN FERRIN

A few pitches up the Royal Arches, we decided, would make a nice climb on this sultry summer afternoon in Yosemite Valley. We'd be down in time for a leisurely dinner and campfire and schmoozing around Camp Four under the August moon.

Ray was the ideal climbing partner for a novice like me. He hadn't fully recovered from his bone-smashing spill on the Himalayan icewall at Nun Kun, and his leg was still in a brace. He still wasn't ready to go back to climbing with the big boys, but he liked keeping his skills honed, and besides, back in the early 70s he was one of the few honchos around Camp Four who was willing and nice enough to climb with women.

Now, the Royal Arches are *very* aesthetic, big curving granite overhangs—like the cloisters of medieval monasteries—on the northeast side of the valley, above the Ahwahnee Hotel. It's a nice walk over there, on the forest path that runs along the bottom of the valley walls.

Okay, so we rope up and Ray leads, placing pins—back then we were still using pitons. I'd follow and pull them out as I moved up the rock face. Also, instead of modern harnesses, we used just a wrapped-webbing "swami" belt about our waists for tying in.

I always enjoyed those times when it was my turn to belay Ray as he moved up, concentrating hard on the task at hand—but something in my mind always went off wool-gathering. I'd muse about how beautiful the place was, those waterfalls plunging down the silver walls into the wildflowers, and how you can remember one kiss on a ledge longer than you can remember a whole relationship. And how climbers could be such bastards and how the good ones had no footsteps. I mean, you could never hear them approaching. But that's another story.

Anyway, we had done about three pitches, and I was tied in to a bolt and belaying Ray from a very minuscule ledge when I realized I shouldn't have guzzled so much lemonade before we started. When he got to the top of the pitch, I decided, I'd take care of the problem before I started climbing. He'd be out of sight above, and I couldn't see anyone below right then. But jeez, the ledge was only four inches wide at most, with solid rock behind it.

I know: I'd let him pull the rope tight and that would hold me in place while I sort of balanced with my toes on the ledge, facing the wall. Got that?

Okay, so he gets to the top of his pitch, yells that he's off belay and ties himself in to start belaying me. "Ready to climb?" he calls a moment later.

"Uh, not quite yet. But I'm on belay. Up rope!"

The rope pulls taut. I turn and face the wall. I yell for him to give me a little slack. So I can get into a comfortable squat, see.

"What are you doing?" he calls.

"Uh, nothing, I'll start in a second. But keep the rope tight."

Swami, buttons, zippers, layers of clothes. Gawd.

Success! Now then . . .

"Hey," comes his voice, "whaddaya doing?"

I was almost finished. "Just a minute! I'll come up soon!"

For some reason he took that as a command to pull up the rope. It was just enough to knock me off balance.

I fell off the ledge, and swung at the end of my rope, on the wall high above the Ahwahnee Hotel, *flagrante delicto,* so to speak.

No shit, there I was.

Then I had to get back on the wall and inch my way up to the ledge from which I'd fallen. Have you ever tried to climb a sheer granite cliff with your pants around your ankles?

Hill Town Horseshoes

JACQUELINE HARMON BUTLER

The hike up the hill through the old village of Collodi was arduous and the morning sun felt hot on my back as I pounded up yet another series of stairs. My friend Claudio was way ahead of me but I stopped anyway for just a moment to catch my breath. I saw a fountain tucked under a nearby fig tree and took a long cool drink and refreshed myself by splashing water on my face. Then, after plucking a couple of the sweet ripe figs, I trudged on.

The climb up the steep and winding stone path through the old town was interesting. There seemed to be a real estate boom going on in this part of Tuscany. Many of the ancient houses had been refurbished and, although the Italian government requires that the exteriors of these historical landmark buildings remain the same, the interiors had been totally modernized. I caught glimpses of some surprisingly elegant living spaces through open doors and windows as I passed by.

The village follows the natural curve of the hillside and is narrow, only two or three houses wide. The path twists through its center, leading straight up the mountain, with turns and stairs to facilitate the walker. There is a small road along the perimeter, with limited parking along the way, giving local residents an option to the exhausting stair-filled path.

Claudio was waiting for me as I rounded the last bend at the top of the village and walked into the San Bartolomeo churchyard. The view from there was beautiful. The Valdinièvole, valley of the clouds, stretched out below, with Lucca to the west and farmlands forming a patchwork quilt to the east. The church, with its wooden sculptures, fifteenth-century frescoes and terracotta statues, was closed tight. We looked around outside but couldn't find anyone who knew when the church would be open. Reluctantly, we headed back down the hill.

We had come to Collodi in search of a special type of horseshoe with built-in hooks that catch on the cobblestone streets. In the days before automobiles, these hooked shoes helped prevent the horses and mules from slipping as they made their slow and dangerous trek down the hills, pulling heavily loaded carts. The area once was filled with important silk mills and the heavy rolls of fabric were transported by horse cart from the factories in the hills to large warehouses near the railroad for processing and, ultimately, shipping. The roads were especially dangerous in winter when the cobblestones were slick with ice.

I had learned about these hooked horseshoes from a friend in San Francisco whose family was from this part of Italy. She didn't know exactly what they looked like but her description intrigued me enough to go in search of them. I thought they must be strange looking and wondered how the horses walked on flat land with them, and if they hurt their feet. When I told Claudio the story of these special hill town horseshoes he, too, was puzzled. He lived on a small farm near Lucca and although there were horses nearby, he had never heard of hooked horseshoes. My Italian is very elementary so, acting as translator, Claudio dutifully asked people we met along the way if they knew about the horseshoes designed for steep hills, where we might get some information and perhaps see what they looked like. People just shook their heads and laughed, saying they didn't know what we were talking about.

As we walked down the road along the edge of town I kept thinking about those poor animals trudging down the steep, slippery roadway and wondered again just what the hooked horseshoes looked like.

Collodi stands midway between Montecatini Terme and Lucca and straggles up the steep hill behind the Villa Garzoni and its extensive gardens. The villa, often referred to as the Castle of the Hundred Windows, is famous as the birthplace of the legendary fantasy character, Pinocchio. Carlo Lorenzini, using the pen name of Collodi, wrote the delightful Pinocchio stories on a well-scrubbed pine table in the kitchen of the villa. Pinocchio's birthday, May 25, 1883, is celebrated in the towns and villages throughout the region.

We wandered down a tree-shaded path to a lovely series of waterfalls that cascaded down the hillside behind the villa. The layout of the garden follows strict post-Renaissance ideals with its rigorous geometrical structures melting into green, the bright spots of flowers; the comic, epic and imaginary elements of statues; the large masks and the glorious fountains.

A gardener clipped away on a small topiary bush in the shape of an elephant and we stopped to ask him if he knew anything about hill town horseshoes. He looked at us and smiled. No, he didn't know what we were talking about, but he directed us to the guard at the Parco di Pinocchio across the road, who, he said, knew a lot about everything.

Piero, the guard, did in fact know a little bit about a lot of things and proceeded to tell us just about all he knew, including the special hooked horseshoes. He actually drew a little picture of one, but no, he didn't know where we could find any. They were too old and he didn't think anyone used them anymore.

The Parco di Pinocchio is an open-air museum designed for children of all ages. The park was built in 1956 and tells the tale of Pinocchio with giant toys, sculptures, mosaics and fountains. The fantastic settings make the tale come alive as you pass by Geppetto, sitting at the end of the dark hole, or the Circus where

Pinocchio changed into a donkey, or the Fairy Child watching as you pass by her little white house.

However, we didn't go into the Parco di Pinocchio. We were hungry by this time and decided to save the park for another day.

We drove east, past Pescia, to the tiny hill town of Uzzano for lunch at the Ristorante La Costa. The restaurant is in an ancient stone farmhouse that has been completely restored. It sits perched on a terrace overlooking groves of olive trees with the fertile valley beyond.

The *padrone* seated us at a cozy table near the windows in the largest of the dining rooms. The sun streamed in through an open window and glittered off a large copper pot filled with flowers in the center of the room. The soft cream-colored walls made an ideal backdrop for an eclectic collection of antique woodworking hand tools. More strange-looking tools hung from the dark wooden beams of the ceiling. On one side of the room was a giant fireplace with a lovely old copper hood. The day was too warm for a fire but I could imagine that the room would be an enjoyable place on a cold winter day. The aroma of grilled meats tweaked my nose as I surveyed the menu.

We began our lunch with a salad of fresh greens and fat, juicy tomatoes, dressed with fragrant local olive oil and balsamic vinegar. This was followed by homemade *pappardelle,* gently tossed with a delicious ragu of fresh porcini mushrooms. Then came a giant mixed grill platter consisting of chicken, steak and house-made sausage, accompanied by a dish of typical Tuscan-style cannellini beans. We chose a lovely Chianti that tasted of blackberries and wild herbs to accompany our feast. And finally, we ate luscious, dark red raspberries covered with sweetened cream.

The *padrone* was a bit stiff and formal at the beginning of our meal but by the time we had scooped up the last raspberry he had become decidedly more sociable and brought a treasured bottle of locally made—and delicious—grappa to our table for us to taste.

Inspired by his friendliness, I encouraged Claudio to ask him if he had ever heard of the hooked hill town horseshoes. Much to my amazement, not only had he heard of them but he had one. I could hardly contain my excitement as he went into one of the other rooms and pulled a rusty old horseshoe off the wall and held it out for my inspection. Claudio took one look at it and laughed in amazement.

"That's what you have been looking for all this time?" he asked. "I didn't realize this is what they look like. I have some of these at home in the barn."

The Accident of Transformation

DANIELLE MACHOTKA

Nestled in my guidebook between two towns in the northern Spanish plains in the region of Navarra, the brief description of the Monasterio de la Oliva ended, "Today, the monks survive by selling their honey, cheese and wine, and by accepting paying guests." Honey, cheese, wine and an alternative to cheap hotels—the combination was too good to pass up. I stumbled through a reservation over the phone in Spanish, leaving my first name only, no credit card number, and my arrival time. The voice on the other end assured me it was more than enough information.

Clouds and rain accompanied me to the gates of the monastery, but something else sat with me as I awaited the arrival of someone who could show me to my room. As my eyes roamed the sitting-room walls, covered with paintings depicting Jesus suffering in ways I had never imagined, the tiniest morsel of misgiving announced its presence with the skip of a heartbeat.

The faint clanging of pots drifted into the room and receded. Not sure what to expect in the way of noises, I was nonetheless astounded by the silence. The caretaker had told me the monks were all at prayer, but that someone would be with me soon. Had I disrupted the service? I cursed my rental car for not getting me to the church on time.

"Danielle?" A hot-cocoa voice said my name in a way that made me feel like a long-awaited relative. I turned to see Padre Felipe, his expression as warm as his voice, striding toward me with his hand outstretched. His brown cassock was secured with a rope belt and his silent shoes made brief appearances with each step. He exuded humility, confidence and complete trust.

"*Buenos días,*" I smiled, accepting his handshake.

"Hello. Welcome." He picked up one bag despite my protestations that it was *pesada,* a word I had mastered lugging my two bulging carry-ons around Spain. But he was out of the sitting room and through the door before I could figure out, "Wait for me!" in his language, and I scuttled to catch up.

Where had I been most recently? Had I come by car? The questions in Spanish flew by as quickly as the two dark hallways that led us to a large back entry with a sweeping staircase. Suppressing the urge to stop and ponder the colorful biblical scenes painted on the walls, I kept my eyes on the barely lit stairs and tried to formulate answers to his questions. He spoke in low tones. I responded in lower ones. My Spanish didn't seem so bad at that volume.

We turned down a long corridor with a row of anonymous doors on the right and large windows overlooking the courtyard on the left. Italian cypress lined the one side of the space, and a rectangle of lawn cradled a lone olive tree. Everything—walkway, lawn, trees—led to the gaping, multi-arched entrance to the cathedral.

At the end of the corridor, we turned into room twenty-one. The window sat wide open in greeting, and I was brushed with a gust of air carrying unmistakable molecules of manure. The sources of both the odor and the basic ingredient for the monk's cheese were nowhere to be seen as I glanced out the window.

The modest room contained a bed, night table, desk and chair. Surprisingly, I had a bathroom of my own. A Bible and the rules of the monastery, both in Spanish, sat on the desk. I skimmed the dozen-or-so rules.

Breakfast at 8:30, lunch at 1:30, dinner at 8:00. From 4:30 in the morning to 9:30 at night there were seven services, three before breakfast. A blurred panic of unknown rituals and painfully early mornings sped through my thoughts.

In making my plans, I hadn't really considered that this was a place of spirituality and worship, not an agricultural cooperative or youth hostel. In my quest for the unusual, I had overlooked the obvious. I read further.

Number seven was written in all caps.

"THE MONASTERY IS NOT A HOTEL. IT IS A PLACE FOR CONTEMPLATION, PRAYER, AND FELLOWSHIP."

Caught in the act of thoughtless tourism.

My overactive-traveler approach—rising early, grabbing break-fast on the run and sweeping through my surroundings, devouring as much as possible in a day—led me to imagine but a few moments of quiet while staying at the monastery. Perhaps a contemplative hour before dinner one night.

When the monks began to take in paying guests, they no doubt envisioned people in need of spiritual rejuvenation, wanting to spend a few days attending services, participating in philosophical and religious conversations with the brothers and rejoicing in the community of faith in which they found themselves. I had, honestly, come with none of those intentions.

And I couldn't fabricate them now. My Spanish barely got me through ordering food and asking directions. Deep ecclesiastical conversations were out of the question. I was seeking nothing from Jesus at the moment. Mute, heathen ignoramus.

My best offering was to alter my plans for the weekend. I could see Tudela and Olite, nearby villages, in an afternoon and a morning. The rest of the weekend I'd stay put, writing in my journal, contemplating, going to services. Vespers sounded soothing. But first, lunch.

I joined a dozen other guests in the communal dining room. Fortunately, everyone else knew what to do, jumping up to the kitchen window to pick up each course as it came, clearing the dishes, folding their checkered cloth napkins and leaving them in the cubby neatly labeled with their room number. I watched, smiled, tried out my Spanish. While everyone appeared to be on retreat, no one showed any signs of expecting the same from me. Perhaps they could imagine no other reason for my presence. Perhaps they were less concerned about it than I was letting myself believe.

The food was remarkably good. A first course of soup, with fresh vegetables and herbs undoubtedly from the lovingly tended monastery garden. Fish with a light tomato sauce and green peppers followed. We crunched on salad and sipped wine. All of it, except for the fish, was the fruit of the monks' labor. On the other hand, we were in the middle of a rock-filled plain, and getting that *pescado* might have required some effort.

A Frenchman two chairs away leaned over and confided that he was a foreigner, too; he offered to speak French with me. François and his wife, Lucia, were my saviors that weekend. He translated the conversations at meals, she showed me what to do during the services, and they always shared their holy water with me—dipping their fingers in it and giving me a "high two," so that I ended up with some of the water on my fingers for crossing myself. Never having been baptized and unfamiliar with the customs, I was too intimidated to reach into the basin myself. We talked about literature, faith, politics and travel. Not religion, particularly, but the communion fed my soul and gave purpose to my stay.

Vespers, the 6:30 P.M. service, began with the cathedral in darkness except for a faint light that struggled in through the high windows—just enough to help us find our seats. Fifteen or twenty worshippers spread out in the pews. We were too few for this Gothic edifice, meant to show reverence by being filled with the faithful, raising their voices above walls that reached for the sky. A lone bell sounded, rung by a brother standing in one of the aisles and grasping a long rope that extended to the belfry. As the lights came up, a line of monks filed in singing. They didn't stop their *a cappella* chants for the entire half hour. Twenty or so peaceful, berobed monks—some who, coming from the kitchen or garden, were taking off aprons and work coats as they entered the church— joined in song with varying degrees of sweet harmony and grating atonality. I tried in vain to follow the prayer booklet given to me, but gave up, closed my eyes and just felt the music.

At the end of the chants, the lights went out again. No one moved. With a click, on came a spotlight, illuminating a small alabaster statue of Mary and Jesus, mounted high behind the altar. I was stunned by the simple beauty of the two serene figures lit up in the enormous dark cavern of the church. As I stared, a feeling of faith arose unexpectedly in the same place that my morsel of misgiving had first appeared. It was an emotion completely free of labels like Catholic or Christian, one filled with generosity of spirit and revelation, populated by open hearts and hands. I had the sense that the world was a good and gentle place, and realized that there was room for me here, too. Here in this building, here at the monastery, here on earth.

Flying Under the Radar

CARLA KING

No, I was not broadsided by a big bad diesel-
dripping coal-flinging blue Chinese truck. I did not slide off the
Silk Route into the Wei River along with the pieces of the shale
cliff that knocked chunks out of the soft new asphalt. I did not
catch a rare Asian flu and I did not fall in love with a goat herder
or decide to shave my head and become a Buddhist nun.

I've been flying under the radar. The traffic cops are more
frightened of me than I am of them, and don't ask me for my
papers, which is a good thing because I don't have any.

After six weeks in China I still cannot identify a hotel building. The word for hotel is a string of characters too long for me to
recognize. Like the word for restaurant and the word for motorcycle parts shop.

I've decided that it's too difficult to do alone, this kind of traveling. . . . the maps aren't quite right, the roads turn into deserts or riverbeds and they leave me exhausted, dehydrated, in a permanent state of low-level panic, like a fever that won't quite go away. Then the bike loses an electrical connection, or I fail to realize that a road is closed, or darkness has come earlier than expected. It never ends, but this is what I've found works best: Stop worrying and go with it. Put yourself at the mercy of the place you land and someone will always save you from considering the whole place a hellhole, the whole race a collection of dead-eyed gaping idiots.

This sounds a little unfair, but let me tell you, the first time I stopped in a remote country village I thought it must be the place they kept all the retarded people. They approached, walking slowly, blank-faced and wooden as daytime living dead—mechanically placing sunflower seeds between their teeth. They spit out the shells; some land on their chins and stay there in the dribble while they gape. More gather, and the air thickens. A hand darts in to work the clutch lever. Another tests the brake lever. The crowd murmurs in approval, and someone enters the circle to bounce on the seat spring.

This happens in every village, so I stop in only the smallest of them, and make sure there are lots of old people around. The elderly protect me. I eat quietly in their shops while they shoo the crowds away. It is not until I return home that I find out that the problem is iodine deficiency and inbreeding. The Chinese are not allowed to move without government permission, so in small villages they intermarry, and intermarry again. It is Appalachia on the other side of the world.

My fortieth birthday passed, a schizophrenic experience involving sledgehammers, coal trucks and a kilometer-long series of Buddhist caves that blew my mind.

The thirty-minute ride to the caves was pure hell. Like playing dodge ball on a motorcycle. Coal trucks dropped skull-sized lumps in every direction to explode onto the road or onto cars or onto me. The broken bits were whooshed by the heavy traffic to the ditches where old women and children collected the largest chunks in burlap bags to use or to sell.

By the time I reached the caves my face and clothes were dusted with coal soot. Still, well-dressed Chinese tourists insisted I pose for photos with them. They ran around excitedly, quickly glanced inside the caves, shouted to one another, flicked their cigarettes on the ground and left within an hour. I hadn't even begun to look around when I was captured by five young Chinese women. They plied me with a snack wrapped in a corn-husk package, a sweet sticky triangle of rice hiding a pitted date. They watched me eat, wiped my face with tissues, powdered my nose and brushed my hair. They chattered and passed around lipstick and a mirror. We took photos. Then they disappeared, leaving me on the wide white sidewalk, wondering where to start.

I spent five hours there, in the Yungang Buddhist Caves, trying to absorb the historic and spiritual importance of the place while Chinese vacationers whirled around, laughing as if it were an amusement park. Here at one of four major Buddhist cave groups in China, I experienced more raw spiritual power than I have felt anywhere else in the world, and I wondered how they could miss it. In the last cave, far from the madness of the central caves with their ice cream vendors and circus camels and astrologers, I was overcome by the stench of urine. Would anyone in Europe piss in the vestibule of a cathedral?

I revisited each cave. Coal dust from the factory across the road collected on the thousands of tiny Buddhas. There are over fifty thousand of them, and they are suffocating.

Datong was the point of no return. Irretrievably far from Beijing and stuck with a bad piston in Inner Mongolia, I was eons from anything the western world might call a city and certainly far from a hotel and hot water. Locals kindly dragged the motorcycle behind a little blue diesel motorcycle truck to the town mechanic, a very young man with a two-year-old daughter and a young wife named Lily. The child climbed into my lap to play with my set of accordion-fold postcards of San Francisco. They had never heard of San Francisco, but by the third day the whole town of fourteen people were all calling me Auntie, and there was a banquet in my honor during which I taught them to say "cheers" when drinking beer. It came out "cherws" and I am sure that this word will be absorbed into their vocabulary and used, with no knowledge of its origin, a century from now. The most difficult task of the evening was to consume all the glistening slices of fatback that flew from their bowls into mine by the amazingly accurate flicks of their chopsticks.

There was nothing to do for three hot Inner Mongolian afternoons, so Lily and I spent them napping on the *kang,* the heated platform they used as a bed. Her soft snore mingled with the roar of blue trucks going by, most of them blowing their horns. So many blue trucks. Big ones, little ones, every single one of them was blue and they would be blue all the way to the Tibetan plateau and back to Beijing. One blue truck after another raced along the smooth asphalt between potholes and breakdowns, carrying their designated loads like a line of dusty, determined ants from the same hill, one accepting the load of another when it became injured or died. Already I felt like a drone on these highways. I'd given some rides in the sidecar to the blue-suited drivers when their trucks broke down.

Even though we had no common language, Lily saved me from thinking of China as one large human ant colony. Lily's flat Han face and features were wide and round, her eyes black and slanted, her body slightly thick. She looked exactly like every other Han woman in my experience. But now I could see that her eyes shone brighter than most, and there was something else about her—I can't say exactly what—that would allow me to immediately pick her out of a crowd.

I was happy here, west of Baotau, in the middle of nowhere. The Inner Mongolian mountains created a protective wall to the south. To the north, land stretched on, forever flat. Days were lazy—taking care of the baby, writing in my journal, taking photos and making Lily laugh by being completely inept at cooking in a wok and washing clothes by hand.

For three days I felt what life would be like here. An endless parade of blue trucks passing by on the highway, beeping at nothing. An endless parade of customers coming to have their motorcycles fixed. An endless series of cooking and cleaning and fetching water from the stream a half mile away. Filling the jugs. Washing the clothes. Preparing the *kang* for sleep. Waking and preparing the *kang* for day. Keeping the baby out of the garbage pile when the sheepherder came around to let his flock pick at the edibles.

The sheepherder was dressed in rags from his head to his cloth-wrapped feet. His staff was a long stick with a curved hollowed-out end that allowed him to scoop up rocks for hurling great distances, to frighten a stray back into the flock. Flies buzzed around him, though he smelled only like dust, like everything else.

I wrote in my journal and waited for the motorcycle parts to arrive from Baotau. The baby clutched the accordion-fold of San Francisco postcards in one hand, displaying the Golden Gate Bridge and the crookedest street in the world and Chinatown and Haight Street. Will she be illiterate like her mother? I thought perhaps, when I got home, I would send her books. But who would read to her? The illiterate learn to communicate using other methods—when Lily looked at me obvious intelligence shone in her bright eyes. What does she think about all day when she stands in the doorway watching the blue trucks go by? The government-run TV station broadcasts a soap opera about the troubles of the wealthy. Another show is an ongoing, highly produced historical saga, and the rest is propaganda. It is all propaganda. None of it has anything to do with Lily's life. Lily stands behind the colored strips of plastic in the doorway and watches the blue trucks go by. Sometimes her husband's customers come in for a cigarette and to gaze at the television while the little repairs to their motorcycles are made, but mostly they stand watching him, engrossed by the mystery of his craft.

By the map, I figured the highway by the Yellow River to be a main trade route with good roads, so on day four I was tearfully on my way, following this route west through Inner Mongolia. Everything became lush and green, the landscape a patchwork of fields tended carefully by peasants in rags and pointed woven hats. I was so happy buying produce from them, and they seemed happy to see me, but at Shapoto the desert suddenly appeared. I never saw it on the map but there it was.

The desert is called the Tenger and the fine yellow sand is moving in on Shaanxi Province like the Sahara is moving in on Senegal, piling up in dunes right into the river. The Gobi sits just over the dry brown mountains to the north. For the first time I was really afraid. How far to the end? How long would it take to cross? The map didn't tell me, so I struck on.

The wheels of the motorcycle disturbed the ribbons of sand that snaked across the road. A lazy hot wind shoved at my right side and the sun glared as if it wished to fall from the sky and obliterate me.

The motorcycle engine overheated, forcing me to stop. I hid under the motorcycle cover from the sun and stinging sand, waited, and started again. There was no traffic for an hour and I wondered if a weather warning had been issued. Did the sign I passed twenty kilometers back read *road closed due to dangerous weather conditions?* Was there a radio broadcast that the truckers listened to? For an hour there wasn't a burro or even a single blue truck carrying coal to the next place. My skin burnt pink from sun and heat and I used the last of my bottle of watered-down tea to hurry the engine cooling.

A herd of camels appeared, shimmering in the heat waves in the hollow by a nearby dune. It could be a mirage, but if they were for real the camel herders would be Muslim men. So I fled, fearing Muslim men in general, with their strident disapproval of women without veils.

The heat rose in waves and the sand covered most of the road and it didn't seem quite real; in fact, I thought I might be in a dream trance, maybe even a state of shock. As I rode on, I thought I saw an ancient woman leading a burro through the storm. It might have been a mirage but she leapt off the road to land in the ditch. The burro only flicked its ear when I brushed it with my left-hand mirror.

The right side of the road was invisible, and so I continued down the middle, looking in the rear view mirror at the woman righteously shaking her hoe after me. Where was she going that she needed a hoe? There seemed to be no use for a hoe for a hundred miles.

The further west I headed, the more bizarre the surroundings and the people. I picked up a hitchhiker on the way to Yinchuan, and then got stuck in what quickly became a nightmare experience in a factory town without women, where men crowded around to see the foreigner. I nearly fainted from heat and stress. But I needed a new clutch cable, and some adjustment to the timing.

I know. I don't have a good history with machines. I don't choose well. I chose local transport when I ought to have imported some fancy precision instrument made for all-terrain, all-weather motocrossing, one of those Paris-Dakar specials from Germany or Japan. But I chose a Chinese motorcycle to take me to these extremes, from fields to deserts to high mountains and back. It is a slow machine, but even so, the trip has been going too fast for my psyche. Perhaps one needs to walk in order to take it all in—the Yellow River, lush and green landscape one moment, nomadic Muslim camel herders at the edge of the desert the next, and not too much farther on, a stream of Tibetan monks falling prostrate every ten steps on their pilgrimage to the Labrang monastery. Rounding a corner I nearly hit three of them but they got up quickly, orange robes all aflutter, and kept walking. Around

FLYING UNDER THE RADAR

the next corner I had to brake hard for a herd of yaks led by a Tibetan woman swathed in brown wool.

After only an hour through pine-covered mountains the Tibetan plateau appeared. The air became thin and cold and even in the sunshine my fingernails froze blue. Can I tell you how I felt then, after having been through that horrible dry desert to find the pine-scented mountains so nearby? It was a relief that came from the gut, the realization that no plan was going to make any sense at all because I hadn't any idea, despite my guidebooks, what was coming next. The only thing to do was to surrender to the resignation that I was not in control, and to simply absorb whatever came next.

The solution? To get to the next place as if it were my only goal. This requires only a small effort. One can always get to the next place.

It consumed me, that thought of "getting to the next place" with its myriad complications that have more to do with instinctual survival than wit or intellect or planning. The path was difficult, but not impossible. This simple phrase—*getting to the next place*—took on great meaning during the six weeks that had just passed. It included all the complications of taking care of the very basics of life—food clothing shelter—plus a tolerance for bodily aches and a mind that looped in only upon itself. This busy mind has no time for mulling over the sacrifices one has made before one boards a jet plane to land on the other side of the world.

Climbing the road to the Tibetan Plateau I reached Xiahe and found other tourists and a hotel room that had hot water between

165

nine and ten at night. During the day I visited the monastery, shopped for trinkets and met other foreigners. Here there were the luxurious moments to think about more than the fact that my thumbs no longer worked properly. About the long stretch of land I'd just crossed, and whether or not to continue the trip south to Burma. At a traveling speed that averaged twenty-five miles per hour because of bad roads and mechanical failures, I decided that no, I couldn't do it. Not by myself. I wanted only to return to my ivory tower on the other side of the world. It was a mistake to come alone. I was definitely on the wrong side of the world, and all the way back to Beijing I was grateful for every little thing because I was headed home home home!

Today, here on the other side of the world, ten thousand rain-drops hit the earth, but there, I was grateful for the ping of cool-ing metal that meant the engine wouldn't overheat. When a stack of rattan containers appeared I was grateful for steamed buns and then I was grateful for somewhere to crouch for a moment in pri-vacy. I was grateful for the gas station that sold the right kind of motor oil and that there were only three broken spokes on the sidecar tire from when I hit that last big pothole, and that the brakes were holding, that there was water to wash my hands and face, and that there was someone to indicate that there was a town with an inn a couple of hours up the road. A couple of hours later I was grateful that I had not been too exhausted to get there. When you travel you are almost never too exhausted, I remem-bered later, just before I went to sleep. Whenever there's no other alternative, you can do whatever it takes to do whatever you need to do.

In sleep my dreams were replays from events of the day. Peasants gather round to stare, so dumbly astonished that they cannot return my greeting. They gather round until there is no more air, and I can't move without bumping somebody's face with my elbow. Why must they be so close to me! "Idiots," I mutter. "Move away!" I shout, and push the ones nearest back so that I can crouch next to the engine. They gather closer, delighted with my performance.

In my dreams there is none of the anger I feel in daytime and I forgive them. I am the first foreigner they've ever seen. I am the last foreigner they will ever see. The only foreigner that they will ever see is a pale-faced green-eyed woman with wispy blond hair who rides a big Chinese motorcycle with Beijing plates. The woman is obviously something that has dropped in from outer space. In my night dream I don't think of what I have done to them by coming here and simply passing through. I'm not responsible for what I've seen. China is China. They've been closed off for a million years, so it is not the fault of the people of the West, at least. Everything that's wrong here is their own fault. I only got a look at it because I was flying under the radar.

Every traffic cop who pulled me over waved me on quickly, in obvious panic, as soon as they saw the blond braid tumble from my helmet. They waved me on before they had to be obligated to admit that yes, they had seen a foreign woman on a Chinese motorcycle and she didn't have the proper papers. What would they do with me? There is no precedent. One of them saluted me repeatedly until I tucked my braid back under my helmet and rode out of sight.

Were they following me, though? Sometimes I wondered. This idea, along with other useless thoughts, followed me closely like an overweight passenger.

"Now remember," one of the Americans advised on the day before I left Beijing, "don't get in an accident, because the Chinese will just stand there and watch you bleed to death. I saw plenty of blood. Truckers in a head-on collision and no one who knew what to do."

What if I died here?

There is something surreal about being so alone in the midst of so many people. One-point-two-billion people. For a long time I felt the fear, but in the middle of my trip it was suddenly replaced by freedom and I was able to let the road take me farther and farther away from the edges of country and the edges of issues and right smack into the middle of everything that was happening around me. In the middle, my head emptied itself of everything but the moment, and the moment contained the cabbage harvest and the sun shining brightly on the tips of green wheat. The moment contained a small forest and the scent of trees being felled, small delicate trees with white bark that looked too fragile to build with.

Most of the road was shaded with bigger trees, their trunks painted uniformly white to four feet up and trimmed with a thin band of red paint. This landscape decoration goes on for miles in China. Kublai Khan had once ordered trees to be planted by the roadside to give solace to travelers. It had become a Chinese habit. Solace was finally mine. Solace was everywhere. Peasants sawed laboriously, sending the fresh green dust into the air. Peasants pulled carts piled high with their green cabbages to market, smiling at the realization of the fruits of their labors. Peasants watered the green wheat. Peasants squatted on their heels and slurped noodles from steaming bowls. I was inside all this, through the forest and the village and then on a road that barely hung onto the sides of terraced mountains. A bee flew up my sleeve. I rubbed at the swelling place on my arm and kept going.

Here, in the shade, is the place I can say that I became a participant and not an observer, when I stopped bothering my mind with the problem of how to send my words away and the problem of the words I might retrieve. Here there was no place for the disturbing bouts of expectations and longings for home that were only exacerbated when seeking an Internet connection.

From now on the ride occupied all the mental space I was willing to spare. Food clothing shelter gas oil adjustments repairs. No room for disturbing thoughts. No room for worry, hope, disappointment, expectation, even joy. A resignation and a real emptiness came to take their place. The kind of emptiness that people go on meditation retreats to seek, using breathing and techniques and rituals that I know nothing about. I can access this space now, when I begin to think too much about how things might turn out, when thoughts just loop around without any possible positive result. What burdens I have placed upon myself! The gamut of emotions tossed around in my head like doomed ships tied together in a stormy sea, banging on each other until they sink, one by one, into depths, hopelessly irretrievable. In the middle I lost them all. Then I was finished. I wanted tea and slippers, and then home.

I had two more hard rides ahead. The first one was an obscure branch of the Silk Route by the Wei River. The road was closed but I couldn't read the sign. I wondered why I was all alone until five hours later I saw a huge scraper completely blocking the road. It would be there until the next day, they said, there was no way to get around it. Huge ditches on each side prevented a drive-around. I would have a ten-hour ride, maybe more, back and around to get to my destination. The men continued working. I walked up and down the road, through a small village, and found a place where, with help, I could get the bike down, around and halfway up. Couldn't they hitch a rope to me and drag me the rest of the way? No. They simply picked up the motorcycle, ten men, and hauled it onto the other side.

Alone again, I was lost in thoughts of Marco Polo and Kublai Khan on their hunting trips—this is where they would have come—until an electrical connection rattled loose. Tightening wires didn't help, the spare coil didn't help, the voltmeter showed everything okay. The truck that picked me up was the only one that ever passed by; it brought the workers home just before dusk. Kindly they dragged me to a town with a hairdresser who braided my hair so tight that my round eyes became slanted like hers, and three mechanics who only made the problem worse. But by the next day I was operational again and off to ride over a huge mountain that, again, wasn't on my map. Dirt road and switch-backs. Riverbeds and road construction. This was my life, day by day, so when I came to Baoji and a truly American-style freeway I was in reverse culture shock. Xi'an was only a two-hour ride at sixty miles per hour down the road, and I made it to the outskirts of town just as the gearbox started rattling. No adjustment would make first or third gear work, so I cruised around town without them and started making arrangements for getting the damn machine on a train home. I had finally had enough.

The terra cotta warriors were a truly awesome site but the tourism industry that surrounded them made me ashamed. I bought a grilled yam from a vendor who charged me ten times the fair price, and I had to literally wrestle the change from her hand. Westerners with fistfuls of play-money shopped and the Chinese took it, either slyly or aggressively. I wandered about in the mid-dle of a thousand transactions, confused, feeling no affinity for the Westerners, who even to me seemed stupid, or for the Chinese, whom I'd traveled amongst for so long, who now seemed mean. I longed for a quiet peasant village, with people who had never seen a foreigner. Everything was different now. What arrogance, to have ever thought I could experience such a trip, and then return to my life unchanged.

In the Realm of the Fire Goddess

LAUREN CUTHBERT

Mounds of shattered lava throw long shadows across the grated path. The sun, its glow muted by a hint of sulfuric cloud, dips toward the crater's rim.

Billows of steam, deliciously warm and moist in the cool air, issue from deep clefts in the jagged landscape. Etched in charcoal one moment, the scene is gossamer white the next. Thin clouds wash across the path. My husband of ten days disappears into the mist.

It is easy, when crunching across the black, steaming expanse of the Kilauea Iki crater, in Hawaii's Volcanoes National Park, to envision the world as it was eons ago when the earth was new, before life grabbed a one-celled toehold and clambered to the surface.

Here on the Big Island the earth really is new. Whereas the other islands in the Hawaiian archipelago are slowly eroding, the Big Island, the chain's largest and youngest, is still growing. For nearly twenty years—the Kilauea volcano has been erupting continuously since 1983—the lava that has flowed to the sea has enlarged the island by more than 500 acres. Unlike the cataclysmic explosion that blew 1,300 feet off the top of Mount St. Helens in 1980, Kilauea's style is far subtler, relying instead on a steady oozing or spouting of lava through fissures to do its work.

The languid clouds lifting skyward merely hint at the violent activity still seething below. A few miles beneath our feet, deep inside Kilauea, where the mountain's base meets the ocean floor, an enormous vault of molten rock rises and falls, causing the surface of the volcano to expand and contract like the lungs of a giant subterranean monster.

That, anyway, is the scientific explanation. Hawaii legend offers a more tantalizing account of the recent activity: Madame Pele, the fire goddess who makes her home on the Big Island, is simply reminding the world of her presence.

Not long after leaving the green lush cover of the crater wall and stepping out onto its dry, wrinkled floor we come upon another couple hiking in the opposite direction. They point out the path across the lava field, its crusted surface just barely smoothed by the passage of untold numbers of waffled soles. Small rocks stationed every few feet on both sides of the track mark a thin trail down the center of the steaming bowl.

"You can't get lost," they say, and then we are alone.

We follow the path, 400 feet below the crater rim, across a meadow of broken, twisted *a'a* lava, which is chunky and rough, unlike the smooth, ropy kind known as *pahoehoe*. In 1959 the crater was a lake of roiling molten lava. Now hardened, it is no less dramatic, its savage beauty frozen in time, lifeless.

Or is it? We marvel at a delicate green sprig that has managed to gain a foothold on life, a preview of the day when this harsh wasteland will be covered with lush ferns and trees like those on the walls surrounding the crater. We are awed. Humbled. The steam closes in. Solitude rises from the cracked, furrowed floor.

Darkness comes quickly in Hawaii and we have dawdled too long in the crater. When we reach the far side of the bowl, the path does its best to fade into the foliage and dusk. A little nervous now, since our flashlight sits useless in the car, we stumble along a few false paths before sighting a small pile of rocks marking the way up and out. When we finally emerge into the empty parking lot from the dense rain forest that enfolds the crater, the moonless sky is only a shade or two short of black.

Not ready yet to let go of Pele's magic, we head down the Chain of Craters Road, 4,000 feet toward the sea. It is strange, after so much solitude, to find ourselves in the midst of so many others as we descend, one in a long line of cars, a twisting row of headlights advancing like an army of glowworms. In the distance, dozens of small blazes flicker like so many campfires on the hillside ahead.

We park near the end of the road, which disappears abruptly beneath a carpet of hardened lava, and join a small crowd gathered atop a hill. We cannot see beyond the jumbled rock, but waves of heat and the stink of sulfur announce Pele at work.

Unable to resist her call, we clamber in single file over the jagged rocks with several others, the beams from our flashlights bobbing wildly across the fractured landscape. We are lucky. In a few weeks this area will be off limits (at least officially), deemed too dangerous for tourist traffic. Friendly voices heading the opposite direction call out the way, though the suggestions are not always the best. A middle-aged man guides his rail-thin mother—who announces to no one in particular, "I simply will not be left behind!"—across a particularly treacherous stretch, then turns back to illuminate our path.

A furious heat greets us as we near the edge of the flow; the air is thick and difficult to breathe. Pools of boiling lava advance on our toes and two small brush fires crackle within arm's reach. We skirt the edge of the fiery field, trying to get as close as possible, but are unable to stand the temperature for more than a moment. A few feet is the difference between extremely hot and unbearably hot, since molten rock can reach a temperature of 2,000 degrees Fahrenheit.

It is the strangest feeling, elating somehow, to be so near a fire that no one makes any effort to put out. What would be the point? The Big Island is still young, and Madame Pele is not yet finished with it.

The superheated darkness leaves people giddy. They laugh among themselves and talk to strangers as if to friends. Perched atop a rock, a man strums a folk tune on his guitar as his four companions sing softly.

A thin, bearded man leans toward us confidentially: "You have to be very careful where you step out there," he announces gravely. Though we have no intention of venturing any further, now or ever, we turn toward him expectantly.

Not so long ago, he says, three young men had tried to cross the lava field, using what appeared to be hardened chunks as stepping stones. "One of them stepped onto one of those." He points to a solid-looking gray patch, seemingly untouched by the raging underground inferno. "And just like that"—he snaps his fingers— "the kid was gone. Swallowed up by the lava."

Perhaps we look dubious. The man picks up a rock and throws it at a small island that juts from a stream of slow-moving lava. The rock misses its target and plops into the molten flow. He throws a second rock. Again, nothing. A third rock lands and sticks. There is a sharp hiss. A red gash appears and the rock sinks from sight. Moments later, the inky surface is as smooth as ever.

Maybe true, maybe not, but we aren't taking any chances. We retreat to the safety of the road, which is only a few days from being further inundated. Away from the searing heat, the night air feels wonderfully cool, though the acrid steam still stings our eyes and lungs.

A quarter mile or so from where the lava plunges into the sea we settle onto a ledge atop the headland to watch the fire goddess in action. Two thick rivers of lava flow like melted butter into the waves below. As the hot stream meets the cool water, steam, dimly illuminated by the fires, rises in a thin gray cloud. It is late, we have a three-hour drive ahead and no prospects for dinner, but never have I felt so happy, so alive.

Suddenly there is a small explosion. A red tongue shoots from the far side of the cliff and with a loud hiss slices the waters below. The crowd cheers. A new course for Pele's fires! Lava spews from the fissure like blood from a wound.

Another blaze ignites, this one at the top of the far headland. As it grows in size it leaves the others behind and slowly lifts into the sky. The all-but-full moon—its face painted a deep yellow by the sulfur gases—reaches the top of the cliff, where it rests a moment before rising toward the stars, dimming their pinpoint lights with its rich, round beam.

The spectacle brings out the primal. A group standing atop a giant chunk of lava behind our seaside perch begins to howl, their silhouettes framed by the glow of dozens of bonfires climbing one atop the other up the side of the mountain.

Cat People Burned My Flesh

ALISON WRIGHT

Pablo, a small wiry Indian with a mischievous grin outlined by a jagged blue tattoo, was one of the most informative shamans that we had encountered during our long journey up the Rio Javari in the Amazon Basin. In more than a month of floating along in the rickety carcass of an old fishing boat, with Peru on one side, Brazil on the other, we had covered hundreds of miles. We were delighted to have finally reached the much anticipated and elusive Matses tribe.

Once ashore, we painstakingly cut our way through the dense jungle with machetes, as sweat soaked through our clothes from the muggy heat. I was along to photograph the trip. Pablo led the way, followed by Tom, an ethnobotanist, and Peter, an anthropologist. We were in search of medicinal plants to bring back to the United States to test their healing qualities.

"These leaves are used topically for treating chicken pox," Pablo informed us. He pointed out various plants, trees and vines. "The sap from this plant is extracted for treating herpes. The heart of palm from this tree is boiled and drunk for treating diabetes. These leaves are applied to the chest for treating a cold." The list seemed endless. The deeper we walked through the green cathedral of trees, I couldn't help but admire the knowledge that the people of the Amazon had of this natural pharmacopoeia, which could possibly house a cure for cancer, diabetes, even AIDS.

The Matses, or Cat People, believe themselves to be descendants of the jaguar. They wear jagged tooth-like tattoos, which outline their jawlines like railroad tracks, to represent the hunting aspect of their nature. Small holes rim their noses where they once proudly wore their "cat whiskers," until informed by Christian missionaries that this was not considered an appropriate practice. Not long ago, polyester gym shorts replaced penis sheaths. The shaman from one of the neighboring Yagua tribes we visited comically shimmied up trees adorned in a ruffle-fronted tuxedo shirt. Who on earth, I wondered, was making these fashion judgments for the native people of the Amazon Basin?

Despite the visible changes, the Amazon Indians still continue to live much as they have for hundreds of years. They retain an intimacy with nature and an appeciation of shared community with their neighbors. As a result, they move through the world with a profound sense of place and purpose. Babies grow up playing in the jungle. Men still hunt wild boar with poisoned arrows and blowguns, and take their dugout canoes and harpoons out onto the river to fish.

On our last night in the village, Pablo invited us to try *sapo,* a sort of slime secreted from a frog's sweat glands. The Matses scrape the stuff onto a stick and let it dry until they're ready to use it. After a lengthy ceremony, they burn it into their skin, inducing uncontrollable vomiting and defecating. Once the body has cleared itself in this way, the Matses believe the hunter receives a clear vision of where the animals lie in wait. *Sapo* is also said to increase stamina and energy.

Clearly, we were that evening's entertainment. The whole village had piled onto our boat to view us entering this altered state. There was excitement in the air as Pablo began heating up the snotty-looking little stick.

"You sure know how to show a girl a good time," I laughed weakly to my companions as Pablo burned through a small layer of skin on each of our arms with a thick hand-rolled cigarette.

As he leaned over, I noticed hundreds of burn marks riding up and down Pablo's arm. "Ah, a *sapo* junkie," I thought. Violently vomiting and defecating in front of fifty-odd people was not high on my list of desires, and I opted for one hit rather than the customary five. As soon as Pablo dabbed the vile-looking ball of slime into the burn, my arm began to tingle with an unrelenting fire.

My heart was racing. I felt as though I were trapped inside a closed, airless elevator. We all began to sweat profusely. Tom's head seemed to be pulsating, or was it my own eyeballs? I flicked the slime off my arm, hoping the nausea would subside, but that only slightly reduced the throbbing in my brain. My stomach was churning, and I tried desperately not to think about the wild boar meat dinner that Pablo's wife had cooked for us earlier that evening. Peter wasn't as successful; I heard him heaving over the side of the boat. These people must have hearts like race horses, I thought, to do multiple *sapo* hits at one time.

Talking became too much of an effort. I crawled over to the bench to lie down. Martha, one of Pablo's wives, flashed me a smile with those giant teeth of hers, outlined in the blue Matses tribe tattoo. That smile was looking pretty darn freaky right then. Martha took my head on her lap, and stroked my hair. Only a half hour earlier I had been laughing and joking with her. Now I was completely subdued in my attempts to quench the nausea and my heart opened completely at her attempts to mother me.

I wasn't hallucinating, but everything suddenly seemed surreal. I found the experience extremely bonding, as all those around me had been in this space before and knew exactly what we were going through. We were certainly the first white folks that they had ever seen partaking in this ritual and we were honored to be invited. Still, I was glad when they eventually seemed to grow bored with our wimpy reactions and filed off the boat.

The next morning my nausea was worse than ever. In addition, ever since the fish lunch the day before, I'd felt as though something were stuck in my throat. Tom, a doctor, looked down my gullet and was amazed to see a fish bone tightly wedged in there, setting off my gag reflex.

"Wow, that's really lodged in there. You're going to have to wait until we get back to Iquitos to numb the area and surgically remove it," he said.

I was desperate. My throat was swollen and constricted. Every swallow was torture. Afraid that I would starve to death, I begged Tom to try to remove the obstruction. Using surgical forceps the length of my forearm, Tom's steady arm managed to extract a spiny bone nearly the size of a cigarette lighter.

With nothing more than a severe sore throat, I was now well enough to join the entourage heading into the jungle. Tom and Peter collected a record twelve plant specimens by late afternoon. Pablo was convinced that their successful hunting trip was due to the *sapo* from the night before. Meanwhile, Martha and Mashu, two of Pablo's three wives, had followed us into the rainforest and Martha beckoned me to accompany her toward a chopping sound in the distance. Giggling, she suddenly raced barefoot through a teeming river of giant leaf-toting red ants marching as though on a mission across the jungle floor. I was apprehensive about crossing their path, even in my heavy hiking boots.

I was astounded when I discovered the source of the hollow chopping noise. There was tiny Mashu, Pablo's second wife, felling an 80-foot tree with a small hatchet. Martha plopped herself down on a fallen log, and I gladly did the same.

We were immediately surrounded by the familiar buzz of mosquitoes. The air was thick with black bugs, all vying for their pound of flesh. Outside for twenty-four hours a day, I had become a human sacrifice, suffering a constant onslaught of insects who insisted on devouring every munchable centimeter of skin in a carnivorous orgy. They were undeterred by military jungle juice insect repellent and dense (hot!) clothing and imperviously seared holes into our oppressive mosquito netting.

Noticing my discomfort, Martha began plucking leaves from a nearby palm, and quickly wove an exquisite little fan. Smiling, she handed it to me—her answer to dealing with the unrelenting pests. This intimate gesture touched me deeply, not only for the obvious usefulness of the gift, but for her shy attempt at communicating.

With swift, flicking hand gestures, Martha then began nimbly crafting a large basket from green palm fronds. Barely flinching, she looked up distractedly as Mashu's large tree came crashing down at her side. Succulent ripe palm fruits now lay at her fingertips, and she quickly began tossing them into her newly formed basket. Pausing briefly, she stooped to cleverly weave a small scoop which served to expedite the process.

Tom's worried call snapped me out of my fascination with the foraging scene.

"Over here with Mashu and Martha!" I yelled.

This sent Martha into gales of giggles and she showed me how the women communicate with *their* men while working in the jungle—a deep-throated moaning sound. In the distance, I heard

Pablo echo a reply. The women and I laughed as I tried to mimic their guttural noises. The men had no problem finding us at that point. Tom joked that he regretted having pulled that fish bone out of my throat.

Ready to head back, the two women hoisted the heavy baskets onto their backs, looping a strong vine around their foreheads as support. Pablo joined us, empty-handed, except for his long machete. His third wife also followed along, carrying their small baby slung on her back, much the same way the other women were carrying their baskets. The baby was sick with a cold and Martha occasionally stopped to pick medicinal plants to stuff into the little girl's shirt next to her chest—the rainforest's answer to Vicks VapoRub.

With three wives, Pablo seemed to have fathered nearly every child in the village (forty at last count), and we were always sure to have a full entourage whenever we went into the jungle to collect plants.

Although Pablo was honored as the village shaman, I was impressed with the knowledge that most of the Indians seemed to have about medicinal plants. Even Pablo's young children were quick to loop vines around their skinny little ankles and shimmy up to the tops of trees for specific plants that they had spotted. Mimicking their father, the boys scurried through the forest with their small bows and arrows in animated delight, shooting at small birds and rodents. The boys had been banned from playing with their bows and arrows for a long time, explained Pablo, because they had a tendency to shoot at all the village dogs and chickens. We looked over to where the boys were sticking their legs deep into the giant red ant hills, daring each other to stay immersed as long as possible.

"Very naughty boys," Pablo stated without much conviction.

At the end of the day we returned to the river and cautiously bathed from the edge of a small wooden raft where the women washed their clothes. The river held threats—crocodiles and *candiru,* small parasitic creatures whose sole purpose on this planet is to swim up one's urethra and lodge there until surgically removed. This was enough to keep us from a full immersion.

Back on the boat we prepared for our long journey back down the Amazon to Iquitos. I finished bagging my rolls of film, while Tom and Peter gloated over their booty, labeling over fifty species of plants they'd collected on the trip.

The sun set, giving the air an illusion of cooling, although the dusk really just marked a change of shift for the ever-present insects. As our boat cleaved the rich chocolate-colored waters, a human-sounding gasp emerged from the depths of the river. I peered over the side. There was a struggle for breath, followed by another. I was worried; was someone drowning? In the descending darkness I could make out small white spouts of spray. It was a school of pink river dolphins, at least twenty of them, leaping in harmonious delight. Playfully swimming in circles around the boat, they emitted a loud chorus of breathless pants in unison. It was as if they knew we were leaving. As if they had come to say good-bye.

The Long Way Home

CATHLEEN MILLER

Certain journeys are best made slowly, such as when leaving one home behind, without another one to take its place. And so it was when my husband Kerby and I decided to sell our Zion, Pennsylvania, farmhouse and return to California in search of the Golden Dream. Our days in Zion had been spent watching our Amish neighbors plow their 300-acre farm with draft horses. The shadowy sketch we had of our new lives consisted simply of camping on a friend's futon in the Castro, a notoriously bohemian San Francisco neighborhood, while we searched for a place to live. We put our belongings in storage and took the train west, feeling it was best to avoid the cultural bends by a slow transition from the cornpatch to the Castro.

While the Pacific Ocean was always our guiding landmark, the path we chose to California was a meandering one, zig-zagging across the continent. I had discovered the Amtrak Explorer Pass, a special fare which allowed us to make any three stops along the way. We plotted our course by choosing the sites we most wanted to visit, then played connect-the-dots. After a farewell celebration in Manhattan, we boarded the train at Penn Station, starting our journey on the Crescent Line, bound for New Orleans.

As we settled into our sleeping compartment, I marveled at its ingenious design. While I'd taken several train trips in the past, this was the first time I'd splurged on the cost of a sleeper. We had the economy version but it had everything we needed, efficiently compressed into a cubicle about four feet wide, eight feet long and eight feet tall, and with a detail I grew to love—a door that could be closed and locked. The compartment contained two seats facing each other, drapery-covered windows, a fold-down table, a pull-down sink, a closet, storage and a bunk bed overhead, which was pushed up when not in use. We discovered that what appeared to be a step to climb up to the bed actually opened to reveal a toilet. We even had our own individual thermostat, as well as a tiny TV with movies, reading lamps and a call button that we would later put to good use.

Outside our window the scenery provided a cross-section of America. We left behind us New York's skyscrapers and crossed the Hudson River to New Jersey's decaying factories—a dismal blur of gray industrial sludge. We traversed the cornfields of Pennsylvania, stopped at Philadelphia's spectacularly restored 30th Street Station, wound through wild mustard pastures where brown and white ponies grazed.

Even though Amtrak absorbed all the regional lines in this country back in 1971, each route retains its unique flavor and the Crescent Line's was definitely a Southern one. Bettilee Hall, the chief of customer service, came by and introduced herself and explained the workings of our compartment. She presented us with two toiletry kits, souvenirs of the Crescent. She also handed us our meal passes for the trip, which entitled us to breakfast, lunch and dinner in the dining car. I stared at her with my mouth agape, because even though I'd made the reservations, I had no idea the sleeper fare included meals.

"How can we get some ice?" Kerby asked. He didn't explain that the ice was for cocktails, which we would shortly dispense from our traveling bar. Our hostess walked over and pressed the call button. "Like this." When a middle-aged woman appeared wearing an Amtrak uniform, Bettilee said, "Miss Diggs, they'd like some ice please." A smile flickered across my face at the old-fashioned use of "Miss" and I realized that we had left Yankee territory.

This impression was reinforced throughout the twenty-nine-hour trip to New Orleans, and by the time I arrived, I felt right at home. I decided that the trouble with plane travel is that while your mind is still in one location, your body is suddenly in another. That first evening we dined on Southern fried chicken in the dining car, and chatted with a young black soldier named Brandon, who had big, shy eyes hiding behind thick glasses. He'd just returned from a tour of duty in Bosnia. Brandon was traveling in coach, which meant he would be sitting up in his seat all night long. He ordered the cheapest thing on the menu: the turkey special and a Pepsi.

He told us the story of how he'd grown up in a Baltimore ghetto. During a high school field trip to the Smithsonian he developed a love of history, particularly military history. The Army had saved him, he reasoned, by teaching him discipline and teamwork. He'd also visited the capitals of Europe, seen sights he never dreamed he'd see. But best of all the Army offered him the chance to pursue his obsession with military history, since it provided soldiers the opportunity to tour battle sites. The government would pay for him to finish his college degree, he said, and afterwards he'd return to Maryland and achieve his goal of becoming a high school history teacher.

"When I came home to Baltimore, I went to visit my old buddies in the ghetto," he said. "I told them to quit complaining about their lives. If you want something to be thankful for, go to Bosnia. At least you guys have running water, electricity, food."

"So what'd they say?" I asked.

He laughed. "They said, 'Man, you're crazy for wasting four years of your life with that Army crap!'"

Around 10 P.M., Miss Diggs made our beds. I climbed up to the top bunk, and was rocked to sleep by the motion of the train. I woke to the morning sun, bright orange in a clear sky, rising over a body of water somewhere in South Carolina. Outside our door was the *Greenville News,* which I carried down to the dining car. I breakfasted on bacon, eggs, grits and the most tender, buttery biscuits I have ever tasted, proof indeed that I was now in the South. I wondered if the biscuits were another product of Miss Ida Mae, a cook the menu advertised had been serving diners aboard the Crescent Line since 1975.

Throughout this leg of our journey, the service was impeccable with the exception of Miss Johnson, the fat, surly commandant of the bar car. She grunted, shouted and refused any customer request, no matter how small. No doubt Miss Johnson had had a distinguished career at the Department of Motor Vehicles before taking her post aboard Amtrak. But when Miss Bettilee Hall entered the bar car I watched our barkeep's instant transformation with amazement, as she began to smile and cajole sweetly, "Is there anything else I can do for you?" I snorted. Anything *else?*

Kerby and I spent a few days in N'awlins and then, after a break-fast at Brennan's which began with brandy milk punch and ended with Bananas Foster, we boarded the City of New Orleans, bound for Chicago. We had al-RADD-y picked up HIGH-ly af-FECT-ed Suth'n AC-cents, so clearly fake they caused our fellow dining passengers to look at us in alarm and question where we were from. That was a difficult question to answer, given our current circumstances. As we launched into a lengthy cornpatch-to-the-Castro explanation, people's eyes widened and the ladies clutched their purses.

We adopted these same gestures at dinner when a retired cou-ple from Michigan tried to enlist us in their multilevel marketing scheme, saying how folks like us would be *perfect* for this sort of business opportunity. No doubt. As the wife waved a business card under my nose and pressed for what I believe in Used Car Salesman School they call "the kill," I suddenly felt FAIHN'T, and had to RUH-ti'e to mah com-PAHT-ment.

At this point I discovered what had become my favorite feature of the sleeper: the door. I had spent many a transcontinental flight with a five-year-old assaulting the back of my seat, while I sat there helplessly wondering how bruised kidneys would affect my future. No amount of eyeball-drilling or sighs that sounded like someone had just popped the emergency hatch phased the mother. She no doubt believed that a reprimand would permanently warp Little Penrod's self-esteem and forever destroy any hope of Harvard Law School. Instead, she placidly flipped through the in-flight merchandise catalogue as my head bounced off the seat in front of me with metronomic regularity.

When Kerby and I escaped from the multilevel marketers, we slid our door shut with joy and locked it. Our attention shifted from dining car intrigues to the ever-changing landscape along the tracks: lush green woods choked with ivy, an alligator in a cage, sharecropper shacks grown over with honeysuckle, worn cotton gins, the dying sun glinting off junkyard chrome and old farm towns that had become ghost towns. The train blasted a warning whistle as we approached the lone crossroads but there was nary a car, a tractor, a wagon, a mule nor a boy on a bicycle in sight.

We changed trains in Chicago and took the State House to St. Louis. At 9 P.M. we arrived in St. Louis and I was very glad to see my brother-in-law waiting to meet us. St. Louis spent $137 million to restore its landmark Union Station and today it features a showplace hotel, restaurants and shops. In the process they decided there was no room for an actual train station, and so exiled passengers arriving by rail to a shack underneath the freeway.

After spending the week in St. Louis, we boarded a train to Kansas City, where we would catch the Southwest Chief to Los Angeles. The journey started out innocuously enough, until we stopped in Jefferson City and 200 junior high schoolers mobbed the train. We hadn't even left the station before they were screaming for the location of the snack bar. Their chaperone slumped into her seat and hollered for them to "give it a rest." This brought about a split-second reprieve before the chaos picked up full steam, and for the next three hours they ran up and down the aisles, shouted, slammed doors, sprayed water from the bathroom faucet, boomed their CDs through portable speakers, blocked the aisles to play cards, shot videos and cleaned out the snack bar like a swarm of locusts gleaning a Missouri cornfield. I began a second-by-second countdown to our arrival.

By 1 A.M., we were on the Southwest Chief, locked in our compartment as the train silently bounced through a sleeping Kansas City. *Wuh-ahhh!* I stared out from the top bunk as the whistle blew farewell to the last of the juke joints and warehouses before we headed out to the open prairie.

In the morning I awoke in Dodge City. I began scanning the horizon for Miss Kitty's Saloon, but instead found Ace Critters, Pizza Hut Carry Out and a Wendy's on Wyatt Earp Boulevard. A billboard proffered a curious invitation: "Visit the Kansas Teacher's Hall of Fame & Wax Museum." The hydraulic brakes squealed to a stop in front of a dilapidated Richardson Romanesque station with the windows boarded shut.

As the train pulled out of town, I realized that during the night we had crossed an invisible border and that—after years of longing—I was in The West again. Lying on the top bunk I gazed at an unflinching blue sky soaring above a limitless plain where cattle ran toward a rainbow. Why does the same sky that spans the country seem so much more enormous in the West than it does in the East? True, part of the answer lies in the unimpeded view from horizon to horizon, but the intensity of color, the cloudless blue, assaults the eye, reverberating in waves—a bold statement which supplicates the viewer.

When the train stopped in La Junta, Colorado, we all got off to stretch our legs. Outside the artificial environment of the sealed car, the land not only *looked* Western, it *felt* Western. I relished this air—light, dry, fresh, weightless upon my shoulders—and suppressed the urge to jump up and click my heels. Crossing the continent by train reinforced for me what a vast, diverse country this is. Who would think Manhattan and La Junta could co-exist under the same sun, let alone under the same government?

In New Mexico I spotted a llama atop a hill, staring at the train. A herd of white-rumped antelope fled our approaching roar. The searing red of the burnt soil was splotched with the cool green of sagebrush, and the adobe buildings blended seamlessly into the dirt from which they were made. Behind the adobes I saw clay beehive ovens. Surprisingly, I also noticed the same anachronistic beehive ovens behind trailers, and I wondered which came first, the trailers or the ovens?

After a week in Hollywood, we boarded the train that I had most anticipated: the Coast Starlight, which follows the shores of the Pacific North to San Francisco. We arrived at Los Angeles's Union Station early, and enjoyed the magnificent architecture of the stunningly restored Mission-style building—a masterpiece of decorative ceramic tiles, gleaming brass and Arts and Crafts furniture.

On board the train a friendly attendant showed us to our car. We would arrive in San Francisco that evening, so we were seated in coach; we carefully selected seats on the ocean side of the train to appreciate the view. However, shortly after leaving the station the attendant came into our car and said there'd been a change of plans and we needed to all move forward to another car. I was just about to take my first bite of the lox and bagel I'd purchased at the station, but wrapped it back up and put it in the sack. We gathered our belongings and trudged to the next car.

I had just unwrapped my bagel again and was salivating with Pavlovian anticipation, when the conductor came through and told us our car was not going to San Francisco, and we would all need to move back where we started from. This time the mutterings of a mutiny rippled through the crowd. Two guys in front of us complained that this car shuffle was getting ridiculous; each time they had to move their backpacks with all their camping gear. The conductor chuckled, unfazed, and continued jovially down the aisle, taking tickets.

A young blond man in his early twenties sat across from us. I had thought several times that he was working very hard to get our attention, and now he chimed in with his complaints. "Hi, my name's Tim," he said, as he got up to shake Kerby's hand.

From the downtown station, the Coast Starlight's route veers west; by the time we reached Oxnard, the tracks were running straight down the beach. Inside the car, talk with our new friend swirled around L.A., music, books, travel. Outside, all manner of life swirled around the aqua Pacific: flocks of pelicans, shiny seals, yellow and orange nasturtiums, mountains of sage and Queen Anne's lace. During our conversation we discovered that at the end of this trip, we would all three be staying in San Francisco, as Tim was heading there to move in with friends as well.

As the clock approached noon, Kerby decided it was time for a trip to the bar car, where he would purchase the Amtrak-preferred beer, Budweiser. "Tim, can I get you anything from the bar?" Kerby offered.

"Uh, yeah, man, I'd love a beer, but I'm afraid I don't have any money," Tim grimaced. I laughed. Now I understood why he was so friendly. I thought back to when I was his age, traveling aboard the train with a couple of dollars in my pocket. I was incredibly friendly to the sailors on board, who bought me beers all the way to Chicago. We played poker in the bar car while one of their buddies played harmonica.

Kerby came back with six Sierra Nevadas and we noted the Starlight's beer selection was an improvement. He said the bartender had been very nervous. "Just promise me if I sell you all these beers you're not going to get drunk and wreck the train like two guys did last week."

We stopped in Santa Barbara for a few minutes and just as we were pulling out of the station, the campers in front of us yelled, "Hey, those are our bikes!" I followed their pointing fingers to see an Amtrak attendant unloading two expensive mountain bikes onto the station platform. "What the hell?! We're going to San Luis Obispo!"

When we stopped in San Luis Obispo, while the campers argued vehemently with the conductor about their missing bikes, a six-foot tall redhead with a broken leg boarded and hobbled down the aisle. She was dressed solely in black, from the tip of her plastic cast to her flat-brimmed ranchero hat, which was jauntily secured under her chin by a leather thong. "Jesus Christ, just let me sit down before I kill somebody," she said to no one in particular. Kerby instinctively knew Red needed a brew, and made another trip to the bar car.

We later learned that the redhead's name was Sunday. For years she'd wanted to take the Coast Starlight, and when she recently broke up with her boyfriend and left Phoenix behind, she decided this was the time. But a major train wreck had forced Amtrak to bus the passengers from Phoenix to San Luis Obispo, and she had missed the best portion of coastal scenery. "This is not the trip I paid for!" she cried. Kerby asked her if she'd like another beer; she said she would, but she was a little short of cash right now. Sunday was heading north to live with a friend and start a new life. My husband returned with another round of Sierras.

Tim explained that he was a little down on his luck, too. Seems he'd been a personal assistant to a big Hollywood star until that star was no longer able to earn a living. Suddenly Tim found himself broke and really wanting to get out of L.A.

"Yeah? Who were you working for?" I asked.

"Robert Downey, Jr." Hoo, boy. That called for another round.

At 8:15 each evening, the Coast Starlight stops at Jack London Square in Oakland before continuing on to Seattle. The San Francisco-bound crowd gathers their luggage and boards an Amtrak bus, which chauffeurs the group across the bay to the Ferry Plaza. Flying across the Bay Bridge in the dark that night, we hopefuls all sat silently, contemplating the single moment of our journey filled with nothing but promise. I caught my breath, as I always do when approaching San Francisco. The city sits by the bay, skyscraper windows twinkling in the cobalt night, the Transamerica Pyramid pointing toward heaven. A red light blinks at its top—acting as a beacon to all us prodigal wanderers.

About the Authors

At age eighteen, **Lisa Alpine** began working in order to finance her travels. She waitressed in Switzerland and picked olives in Greece, explored the Amazon River and created a South American import company (Dream Weaver Imports), two retail stores and a wholesale business. When her son Galen was born eighteen years ago, Lisa decided to settle in Marin County, California, and become a travel writer. Since their first trip to Morocco when he was eight months old, Galen has been her most frequent travel companion, whether singing nursery rhymes to lounging lions in Kenya or snorkeling with giant squid in Fiji.

Lisa has contributed to the *Los Angeles Times,* the *San Francisco Examiner, Physicians' Travel and Meeting Guide,* the *Atlanta Journal/ Constitution, Parenting* and *Specialty Travel Index.* She writes a monthly column for the *Pacific Sun* and teaches at the Writing Salon in San Francisco. When not wrestling with words, Lisa dances, leading her Dance Weaver workshops all over the world. (www.danceweaver.com)

Jacqueline Harmon Butler saw the film *An American in Paris* at an impressionable age and dreamed of being an artist and living on the Left Bank. Instead, she spent her formative years hanging out in San Francisco's North Beach with the Beat Generation, wearing a black beret, writing stories and painting. It wasn't until she had married, divorced and raised two children that she went to Paris. It was love at first sight.

Jacqueline is an award-winning writer and has contributed to many newspapers and magazines, including the *San Francisco Examiner,* the *Los Angeles Times,* the *New Orleans Times Picayune, Medical Economics, True*

Love, Mocha Memoirs, Virtual Italia, My Backyard and *Travelers' Tales*. She is currently working on a novel about a woman of "a certain age" who travels to Italy and falls in love with a much younger man. When not traveling and writing stories, she is a sales executive in the fashion industry.

Lauren Cuthbert turned three in Japan, four in Las Vegas, nine in Mexico and sixteen in Spain. Thereafter, she determined to spend as many birthdays as possible on the road, subsequently adding Italy, Greece, Hong Kong, Thailand, Burma and Costa Rica to the list. After graduating from the Columbia University Graduate School of Journalism in 1989, Lauren moved to Hong Kong, where she worked for two years as a reporter for the *South China Morning Post* and traveled extensively throughout Asia. Her travel stories have appeared in the *San Francisco Examiner*, the *Atlanta Journal/Constitution*, the *Fort Lauderdale Sun/Sentinel*, *World Traveler* and other publications. She has also worked as a travel writer and editor for the online sites GNN.com and Worldview Systems. When not writing about travel, she works as a medical and science reporter.

Lynn Ferrin was nine years old and knew she was in the wrong place: Texas. One day her father came home and announced the family was moving to Kuwait and her traveling—and writing—career began. Since then, she has roamed the planet by foot, horseback, kayak, canoe, ship, plane, train and camel. Currently a freelance travel writer, Lynn was an editor and writer for thirty-seven years for *VIA*, membership magazine of the American Automobile Association in California, Nevada and Utah. In addition to hundreds of articles in *VIA*, Lynn has been published in major magazines and newspapers in the U.S. and abroad, including *Travel and Leisure, Ms.,* the *San Francisco Chronicle,* the *New York Times,* the *Los Angeles Times, Newsday,* the *Globe and Mail* and the *Dallas Morning News*. Her specialty is writing about adventure travel and public lands. She has lived in a cluttered hillside cottage in San Francisco for more than thirty years.

Carla King started writing about travel in 1988 during a technical writing job in Lyon, France. In 1993 she penned a mountain-biking guide to the Alpes-Maritimes, then left for a four-month bicycle trip through West Africa. Since then, she's published stories about motorcycling, bicycling, kayaking, scuba diving and travel technology in newspapers, magazines and anthologies, including the *San Francisco Examiner, Rider, Dive Travel, Rough Guides' Women Travel, In Search of Adventure* and *Travelers' Tales*.

In 1995 Carla pioneered the art of the realtime Internet travelogue with the popular *American Borders* dispatches, followed up by *China Road* (1998) and *Indian Sunset* (2000), on each trip riding a different vintage motorcycle.

For her work in travel, technology, and the art of motorcycle maintenance, Carla has been featured in publications from *Escape* to *Cybergrrl @ Work,* and radio and television shows ZDTV's *Internet Tonight,* Boston's *The Wild Wild Web* and the BBC. (www.carlaking.com)

Jennifer Leo is a fourth-generation Chinese-American, a theme that frequently recurs in her writings, whether she's traveling to Vegas to take a chance at the craps tables or scuba diving among sharks in Southern Australia. During her six years at Travelers' Tales publishing house, Jennifer co-edited the Travelers' Tales anthology *A Woman's Path: Women's Best Spiritual Travel Writing.* Her stories have appeared in *A Woman's Passion for Travel, The Adventure of Food, BootsnAll.com* and *WhoopWhoop,* an Australian travel magazine. At this time Jen is on a year-long adventure, gambling her way around the world as research for her book *Looking for Luck.* (www.bootsnall.com)

Danielle Machotka's parents took their two daughters to visit family in the "old countries" when Danielle was six. Thus began a cycle of travel and wanderlust that has been with her all her life. At some point, Danielle realized she wanted to write about the experiences of being a blonde woman traveling alone in Bangkok, about preserving the landscape in Cinque Terre and staying in a Trappist monastery in rural Spain. So to save the ears of her friends and family, she began recording her adventures on paper. She's wandered around Europe, the South Pacific and Southeast Asia, and written about it for the *San Francisco Examiner*, the *Denver Post, Transitions Abroad, Reno Air Approach, Adventure Journal* and *Big World Magazine*.

Linda Watanabe McFerrin has been traveling since she was two and writing about it since she was six. A poet, travel writer, novelist and contributor to numerous journals, newspapers, magazines, anthologies and online publications including the *San Francisco Examiner,* the *Washington Post, Modern Bride, Travelers' Tales, Salon.com* and *Women.com*, she is the author of two poetry collections and the editor of the fourth edition *Best Places Northern California* (Sasquatch Books, 2001).

A winner of the Katherine Anne Porter Prize for Fiction, her work has also appeared in *Wild Places, In Search of Adventure* and *American Fiction*. She is the author of a novel, *Namako: Sea Cucumber* and a new short story collection, *The Hand of Buddha*.

Linda also teaches and leads workshops in fiction and creative nonfiction at colleges, universities, literary programs and booksellers across the country. (www.lwmcferrin.com)

Pamela Michael's books include *The Gift of Rivers, A Woman's Passion for Travel* and *A Mother's World: Journeys of the Heart*. In her youth, she crossed the U.S. several times, by thumb, rail, bus and car, sometimes with her infant son in tow (and often her Irish wolfhound as well). She didn't leave the continent until she was over forty, but has made up for lost time, visiting over thirty countries in the last decade. In 1997, she won the Book Passage Travel Writers Conference grand prize for her story, *The Khan Men of Agra*. Also a radio producer, Michael hosts a travel show on KPFA-FM in the San Francisco Bay Area, and wrote and produced a nationally broadcast, four-part series on Buddhism narrated by Richard Gere. She is director and co-founder (with Robert Hass) of River of Words, a nonprofit international children's arts and environmental education organization. She lives in Berkeley, California, with her Tibetan terrier, Yeti, whom she considers the perfect menopausal companion.

Cathleen Miller is the co-author of the international bestseller *Desert Flower*, published in sixteen countries. *Desert Flower* is currently being made into a feature film by Rocket Pictures, U.K. Cathleen's forthcoming memoir, *Back to the Country*, describes one of her many absurd life experiments—namely her move from Pacific Heights in San Francisco to commune with her Amish neighbors in Zion, Pennsylvania. Her work has appeared in the *Washington Post,* the *San Francisco Chronicle,* the *Chicago Tribune,* the *Denver Post, Cimarron Review, Old House Journal* and *Travelers' Tales San Francisco.* She received her MFA in Creative Nonfiction at Penn State and currently teaches in the graduate writing program at the University of San Francisco.

Christi Phillips began writing about travel after living in Moscow in 1991. Over the years she's been a screenwriter, magazine reporter, guidebook author, editor and ghostwriter, and has contributed to numerous publications, including the *San Francisco Examiner*, the *Richmond Times-Dispatch*, the *Toronto Star*, the *Rocky Mountain News*, *Greece Travel Magazine* and *Travelers' Tales*. She is the co-author of *Vodou Visions: An Encounter with Divine Mystery* (Random House) and has recently completed a memoir, *Red Caviar, Black Caviar: The Misadventures of an American Woman in Moscow*.

Since receiving her first camera and journal at ten years old, **Alison Wright**, a freelance photojournalist and writer, has traveled from the Arctic to the Amazon documenting the traditions and changes of endangered cultures in remote areas of the world. After two years living out her cowgirl dreams in the outback of Australia, Alison spent four years in Nepal capturing the plight of children there for UNICEF and other aid organizations. In 1993 she received the Dorothea Lange Award in documentary photography for her photographs of child labor in Asia. Documenting Tibetan life in exile has been her project of passion for over a decade. Alison's photographs have been showcased at the Smithsonian Institution. Her published works include *The Spirit of Tibet: Portrait of a Culture in Exile* (Snow Lion) and *A Simple Monk: Writings on the Dalai Lama* (New World Library), as well as many other books and periodicals worldwide. (www.alisonwright.com)

Acknowledgments

"Swiss Squeeze" by Pamela Michael. First published in *The Gift of Rivers* (Travelers' Tales). Copyright © 2000 by Pamela Michael.

"Learning to Breathe" by Alison Wright. First published in *Outside*. Copyright © 2001 by Alison Wright.

"Maddening Madagascar" by Lisa Alpine. First published in *I Should Have Stayed Home* (Book Passage Press). Copyright © 1994 by Lisa Alpine.

"On Pleasures Oral" by Linda Watanabe McFerrin. First published as "Giving Good Gnocchi" in *Salon Travel*. Copyright © 1997 by Linda Watanabe McFerrin.

"Chinese Like Me" by Jennifer Leo. First published in *A Woman's Passion for Travel* (Travelers' Tales). Copyright © 1999 by Jennifer Leo.

"Progressive Supper" by Jacqueline Harmon Butler. First published in *The New Orleans Times Picayune*. Copyright © 1997 by Jacqueline Harmon Butler.

"The Place of Wild Tortoises" by Lynn Ferrin. First published in *Great Escapes (San Francisco Examiner)*. Copyright © 1990 by Lynn Ferrin. Reprinted by permission of the author.

"Taking Dedecek Home" by Danielle Machotka. First published in *Big World Magazine*. Copyright © 1997 by Danielle Machotka.

"The Khan Men of Agra" by Pamela Michael. First published in *A Woman's World* (Travelers' Tales). Copyright © 1995 by Pamela Michael.

"The Art of Darkness" by Christi Phillips. First published in *The Richmond Times-Dispatch*. Copyright © 2001 by Christi Phillips.

"It's a Man's World" by Lynn Ferrin. First published in *No Shit! There I Was . . .* (ICS Books) in 1994 and in *Not So Funny When It Happened* (Travelers' Tales) in 2000. Copyright © 1994 by Lynn Ferrin. Reprinted by permission of the author.

"Hilltown Horseshoes" by Jacqueline Harmon Butler. First published in *Virtual Italia*. Copyright © 1999 by Jacqueline Harmon Butler.

"The Accident of Transformation" by Danielle Machotka. First published in *The Denver Post* and *The Philadelphia Inquirer*. Copyright © 2000 by Danielle Machotka.

"In the Realm of the Fire Goddess" by Lauren Cuthbert. First published in the *San Francisco Examiner*. Copyright © 1998 by Lauren Cuthbert.

"The Long Way Home" by Cathleen Miller. First published as "Savoring America by Rail" in *The Washington Post*. Copyright © 1999 by Cathleen Miller.

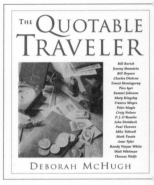
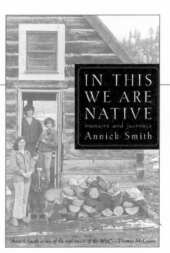